MORL
LOCAL HEROES

ADAM HART-DAVIS presents *Local Heroes*. A freelance writer and television presenter since 1994, he previously worked for YTV as a researcher and producer, devising both *Scientific Eye*, the most successful school science series on television, and *Mathematical Eye* (1989–92), as well as five programmes on Loch Ness for the Discovery Channel (1993). He is also a science photographer, and his photographs have appeared in a wide selection of publications. He has written eleven books, including *Thunder, Flush and Thomas Crapper* (1997), *The Local Heroes Book of British Ingenuity* (1997) and *Amazing Math Puzzles* (1998). He lives in Bristol, and travels by bicycle. . . .

PAUL BADER is the owner and managing director of *Screenhouse Productions Limited*, a television company which specialises in popular science programmes, and is producer and director of *Local Heroes*. He previously worked for YTV, producing medical, health and science programmes for the ITV network and for Channel 4. Among other programmes, he has worked on *Discovery*, *The Buckman Treatment*, *The Halley's Comet Show* and *On the Edge*. He lives in Leeds, and travels by car.

MORE
LOCAL HEROES

ADAM HART-DAVIS
and PAUL BADER

SUTTON PUBLISHING

First published in the United Kingdom in 1998 by
Sutton Publishing Limited · Phoenix Mill
Thrupp · Stroud · Gloucestershire · GL5 2BU

British Library Cataloguing in Publication Data
A catalogue record for this book is available from the British Library

ISBN 0 7509 1797 0

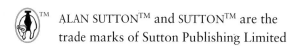

ALAN SUTTON™ and SUTTON™ are the
trade marks of Sutton Publishing Limited

Typeset in 10/14 pt Sabon.
Typesetting and origination by
Sutton Publishing Limited.
Printed in Great Britain by
Ebenezer Baylis, Worcester.

CONTENTS

ACKNOWLEDGEMENTS

The authors would like to thank the following individuals and organisations who generously provided illustrations for this book:

Armagh Observatory, p. 36; Bradford Libraries, p. 56; British Cement and Concrete Association, pp. 117, 118; Gloucester Folk Museum, pp. 67, 68; Hulton Getty Picture Library, p. 130; ICI, p. 3; Kings Lynn Museum, pp. 27, 28; Mary Evans Picture Library, pp. 11, 21, 33, 53, 54, 64, 66, 70, 75, 98, 121, 126, 136, 140; Royal Engineers, pp. 127, 128; Science and Society Picture Library, pp. 84, 105, 106; Screenhouse Productions, pp. 17, 29; The Arkwright Society, pp. 88, 90; The Guildhall Library, p. 115; The National Maritime Museum, Greenwich, p. 7; The Royal Society, p. 78; Valerie Doodson, p. 14.

The following photographs are copyright the authors:

Adam Hart-Davis, pp. 9, 20, 31, 48, 60, 61, 74, 101, 102, 112, 116; Paul Bader, pp. 4, 16, 25, 30, 34, 41, 51, 52, 58, 62, 83, 85, 99, 119, 132, 133, 142.

INTRODUCTION

Local Heroes carries on! As we write this, in the soggy summer of 1998, we are just about to finish shooting the fourth BBC2 series. By the time this book is published we shall have made a total of forty-two programmes, covering about 200 heroes. Our hunt for them has taken us from Shannon to Syracuse, and from Aberdeen to Alexandria, and has led Adam and his bikes up Ben Nevis and Mount Etna, along many moors and beaches, and even 20 feet under water, where riding a bicycle is almost impossible without a heavy lead weight on the handlebars.

This year has seen the usual crop of location disasters: Adam has been playfully nudged in the ribs by colossal shorthorn bulls; dropped in more kinds of water than he cares to remember; cajoled up mountains that seemed to get higher with every aching step; and balanced precariously on precipices and arches of home-made bricks. The weather has not been kind; we have scarcely seen the sun, and snow fell as we filmed by St Paul's Cathedral on 26 June!

Two things have become even clearer in the last year. First, the connections between our heroes gradually develop. Many of them must have known one another, and as we read more and more about them we discover all sorts of hidden links. For example, James Watt would probably never have thought of using a

separate condenser for the steam engine if he had not known Joseph Black, expert on latent heat; nor would he have been able to make his steam engine work without the brilliant cylinder-boring of John 'Iron-mad' Wilkinson. Watt may have been the first person to suggest in public that water was a compound of oxygen and hydrogen – or dephlogisticated air and inflammable air, as he put it – but he had almost certainly heard of Henry Cavendish's results, which were communicated to Joseph Priestley, a friend of Watt's at the Lunar Society.

Secondly, the more we search, the more ignorant we find we are. Every new library, every letter from a viewer suggesting a new hero, finds us unaware of some whole field of scientific thought. We are merely scratching the surface of scientific and technological history, and depend largely on the real experts to whom we so often go for advice.

Of the stories in this book, some are old, old favourites. John Harrison's fifty-year struggle to solve the problem of longitude and persuade the Board of Longitude to give him his just reward is one of the most powerful of all, but we dearly love the absurd eccentricity of Thomas Romney Robinson with his rockets, and Lewis Fry Richardson with his parsnips; sometimes we wish we could have been scientists doing such wild experiments! And we stand in awe of the pioneers whose ideas were so colossal they really changed our way of life, such as Thomas Newcomen with the first working steam engine and Richard Arkwright with his water-frame; these men started the industrial revolution. In this book you will also find the origins of the telephone, the fax machine (thirty years earlier!), the television, and many other weird and wonderful devices.

While making the series, Adam had most fun with the heroes of transport, because he had to ride peculiar bicycles, tractors, a hansom cab, a kite-powered buggy, and even a tank. The most scary thing, apart from trying to balance on a high bicycle, was setting sail in a home-made submarine, luckily only in a swimming pool. Perhaps the most satisfying was ploughing a field near Belfast with a 'Wee Fergie' – a beautiful little tractor that makes you feel at home after five minutes in the saddle.

Anyway, here are another fifty-four heroes, loosely grouped in themes, some serious tales and some frivolous; we hope you enjoy them as much as we do.

Adam Hart-Davis & Paul Bader
July 1998

AMAZING
MECHANISMS

From the stone axes of the early hominids to the computers – and the mousetraps – of the late twentieth century, ingenious devices have always been symbols of the intelligence of the human species. No other species builds machines. And as Richard Gregory has pointed out, machines actually enhance our intelligence. For example, knowing you have a pair of scissors allows you quickly to work out how to cut a piece of string or to open an impenetrable package; you don't have to start from scratch with every problem that arises.

Here are the stories of some weird and wonderful mechanisms, their origins, and the people who invented them.

1. William Bickford's Safety Fuse

2. John Harrison's Marine Chronometers

3. Charles Babbage's Calculating Engines and

Ada Lovelace's Programmes

4. Frank Hornby and Meccano

5. Arthur Doodson's Pendulums for Tide Prediction

6. Barnes Wallis and the 'Impossible' Bouncing Bombs

7. Alastair Pilkington's Floating Glass

1. WILLIAM BICKFORD'S SAFETY FUSE

For thousands of years Cornwall has been a mining area; all sorts of useful minerals have been dug out of those tough hills. At first the miners used picks and shovels, but as the demand increased and the stakes got higher they turned to gunpowder. Large quantities of rock can be quickly shifted with an explosive charge.

However, the problem about setting off any explosion safely is to do it without blowing yourself up. The simplest method is to lay a trail or 'train' of gunpowder along the ground from the main charge for about 30 yards; this will take between five and ten seconds to burn. Then you light the end of the train and either crouch behind a large rock, or sprint off to a safer distance, while the fire sputters and fizzes all the way along the train and ignites the main charge. At least, that's the theory. However, there are several difficulties with powder trains.

Quite often the flame stops, and doesn't set off the explosive; this is called a 'hang-fire'. Sometimes sparks jump ahead along the train, so that it goes too quickly and you blow yourself up. The most dangerous is when you think it's stopped, and you go to have a look – but in fact it was just having a rest and you get blown up.

The weather often prevents powder trains from working. Wind can blow away some powder, leaving gaps in the train, before you have a chance to light it. When the ground is wet or there are puddles or perhaps a stream to cross, you can't lay a train because the gunpowder gets wet easily, and then won't burn. The slightest rain rules out the use of powder trains completely.

And there is a more fundamental problem. Miners often want to place the main charge in a hole they have drilled in a wall of rock. There is no way of laying a trail up a cliff, or into a hole drilled into rock – especially as the hole has to be filled to contain the blast.

Goose Quills

For many years shot-firers used goose quills to make a fuse. Fill each hollow quill with gunpowder, then push the point of one into the back of the next, and push together as many as you need. In theory the powder will burn along each quill, then burn through the point and light the powder in the next one.

The quills protect the powder from wind and damp, and in principle you can lay a goose-quill fuse up a cliff and into a hole in the rock. Goose-quill fuses were fairly convenient but not entirely predictable. The main trouble is that quills are rather delicate. When the shot-firer rammed rubble into the hole containing the fuse, he often broke a quill or two. This might cause the fuse to fail, or let some powder escape which set off the charge too soon.

Often there was simply a break in the gunpowder train, causing a hang-fire. After waiting till he thought it was safe the shot-firer came back, only to find the quill had actually been smouldering slowly, the flame had just carried to the other side of the break, and the charge exploded, causing injury or death.

The Safety Fuse

William Bickford had an inspiration in a rope factory that did away with all this, saved hundreds of lives, and was in use for

150 years – though he didn't make a penny. He was born in January 1774 in Ashburton in Devon, and went to Truro as a currier (that's a chap who prepares leather), but he wasn't very successful so he moved to Tuckingmill near Camborne.

Tuckingmill was right in the middle of the most significant mining centre in the country. Bickford had no connection with the mining industry, but he was apparently 'particularly distressed' at seeing the results of blasting accidents, and he set his mind to the possibility of a safety fuse. His first idea was to put the main explosive in a cartridge made of parchment, and to attach a small parchment tube containing powder as the fuse. The principle was rather like that of the quills – but sadly the practice was just as unreliable.

One day in 1831 he visited his friend James Bray who owned a rope factory in Tolgarrick Road, and as they chatted Bickford had an inspiration. In those days rope was made in a rope-walk; the rope-maker first tied one end of each strand to the wall, and then walked backwards while twisting the separate strands together to make the rope. As he watched the rope-maker, William Bickford realised that he might be able to adapt this process to make a fuse.

Bickford watched fascinated as the strands of rope came together, and noticed that they always twisted round a narrow space in the middle. This disappears as the rope is tightened, but Bickford wondered whether he could fill the middle of the rope with gunpowder. If he could do so, he would get a convenient fuse, and a simple and continuous method of manufacture. He designed a machine to do the work, and patented it later the same

Advertisement for Bickford's Safety Fuse. The fuses used two threads running through the centre to carry the flame over any breaks in the gunpowder trail.

year, 1831. The machine wound strands of rope around a central core of gunpowder. Then it wound another layer in the opposite direction in order to prevent the rope untwisting. Finally the rope was varnished to make it waterproof.

His invention was brilliant in its simplicity. When one end was lit, the rope safety fuse would burn steadily along its length at a rate of perhaps one foot every ten seconds. It hissed and spluttered and sparked, but it never went out. Because it burned at a steady rate, the shot-firer could simply cut off the right length to give himself time to escape – say six feet if he wanted it to take a minute to burn. The safety fuse consumed much less powder than a powder train, it burned much more slowly, and it was far more reliable. It was not affected by weather, and would even burn under water if the fuse had to be laid across a stream.

Even though the miners disliked having to buy safety fuse, they were quick to

The Bickford Smith fuse factory in Tuckingmill. By 1930 one year's output of safety fuse would go four times round the earth.

realise that its reliability made it much the best – and safest – fuse available. In its first year, the Bickford factory in Tuckingmill made 45 miles of fuse; this is a colossal amount when you consider that it was used in quantities of only a few feet for each blast. A hundred years later, in 1930, the same factory, somewhat enlarged, made 104,545 miles of fuse.

Over the years various specialised fuses were developed, suitable for use in specific conditions, such as: waterproof fuse for use under water, and extra-safe fuse which did not make sparks, for mines where explosive gases were present. Fuses had coverings of various colours to show up on different sorts of rock. However, the basic process of making safety fuse is essentially unchanged to this day; Bickford's was one of those brilliant inventions that fills a want so precisely that no one can improve it.

Sadly William Bickford knew nothing of this success. He became paralysed in the year following his great invention, and died two years later in 1834, just before the fuse factory opened for business.

The remains of Bickford's factory, beside the main cross-roads in Tuckingmill, is now occupied by a number of small businesses grouped around a courtyard.

2. JOHN HARRISON'S MARINE CHRONOMETERS

A few miles from the southern end of the Humber Bridge stands an elegant house called Brocklesby Park, the home of the Earl of Yarborough. The stable block no longer holds many horses, but its little tower houses a magnificent clock, built in 1724 and still keeping perfect time today. The man who made it was a village carpenter called John Harrison.

Every part of the Brocklesby Park clock seems to embody a clever idea. The whole thing is made of wood, even the cogwheels. We would have expected them to be wearing out after 275 years of continuous running, but Harrison made the cogs of hardwood, with the grain running up each tooth for maximum strength, and there are several anti-friction mechanisms to avoid abrasion of the wood. The clock is a remarkable machine, and the man who built it was equally remarkable.

John Harrison was born in 1693 in a small village on the Nostell Priory Estate near Wakefield in Yorkshire. His father Henry was a carpenter on the estate, and also repaired clocks. In 1700 the family moved to Barrow-upon-Humber, close to where the south end of the Humber Bridge is today. John helped in his father's workshop and became fascinated by machines on wheels. He was never able to express his ideas clearly in writing, but he was so interested in science that he borrowed a copy of the lecture notes on natural philosophy by Professor Nicholas Saunderson at Cambridge, and copied them all out, including the diagrams.

On 22 October 1707 there was a naval disaster. Admiral of the Fleet Sir Clowdisley Shovell, returning home from the Mediterranean, made a navigational mistake and in the middle of the night sailed full tilt into the Scilly Islands. Three ships were wrecked, 200 men drowned, and Sir Clowdisley himself, after staggering injured through the surf to the shore, was murdered by a woman for the ring on his finger.

Queen Anne was appalled that such an experienced seaman was unaware of his position. Her advisers explained that the problem was about longitude. When you are out of sight of land, finding out how far north or south you are – your latitude – is fairly easy as long as you occasionally see the sun or the stars. But finding out how far east or west you are – your longitude – was a difficult problem, and no one had yet found a solution.

So, in 1713, Queen Anne proclaimed a reward of £20,000 for anyone who could solve the problem of longitude or, more precisely, could find a method by which sailors could determine their east–west position to within 30 miles.

This was a massive amount of money, and dozens of suggestions were sent in, some of them more sensible than others.

One idea was to anchor a ship every 100 miles across the main oceans. Each of these ships would fire a cannon every day exactly at noon. Then any other ship within sight or hearing would be able to work out its position. Another suggestion was to supply each ship with a wounded dog. The bandage from the wound would be removed and kept on shore. At precisely noon every day some trusted person on shore would sprinkle on the bloody bandage a little of the famous 'powder of sympathy' discovered in the south of France by Sir Kenelm Digby, and the animal, feeling the psychic connection to its injury, would howl. Then the sailors would know exactly when it was noon in England. No one was quite sure whether this would work when the animal was thousands of miles away, and it was callously suggested that the animal might have to be wounded several times during the course of a long voyage.

The Astronomer Royal, Nevil Maskelyne, believed that the longitude problem would be solved by astronomy, using precise tables of the eclipsing of the moons of Jupiter, or some such data. Since he was a member of the Board of Longitude, whose duty it was to award the prize, the Board came to be rather biased in favour of an astronomical solution.

However, when word of the prize reached Barrow, John Harrison believed he could solve the problem with a simple clock, adapted for use at sea – a marine chronometer. His idea was to use time to measure longitude. Suppose your watch is set to Greenwich time. At noon the sun will be at its highest point in the sky. Now go across the Atlantic: at noon in New York the sun will again be at its highest point in the sky, but your watch won't say noon, it will say about five o'clock. In other words, when it's noon in New York it's five o'clock in London; thus, New York is five hours behind London. Or in other words, it takes that long for the sun to cross the Atlantic.

The sun takes twenty-four hours to go round the world, so New York is five twenty-fourths of the way round the world. Obviously that's one way of measuring how far west New York is from Greenwich. If you are navigating a

ship, you need to be much more accurate than that, because if you were one minute wrong, then you'd be 17 miles out east or west; you could easily miss a small island – or crash into the Scillies. But by 1730 John Harrison reckoned he could make a clock that would be accurate to within one second a month, and with that he was sure he could win the prize.

He designed one in 1728 and took his drawings to London, but was advised to make a model to convince the Board of Longitude. So he went back to Barrow and started building. Seven years later he came back with a huge clock, standing about four feet high, with amazing springs bouncing out of the sides like arms.

He asked for a trial run, and the Board sent him on a voyage to Portugal and back, even though their own rules had specified the trials should take place on voyages to the West Indies. While he was in Portugal the captain died; the mate was delighted to have Harrison's assistance in navigation during the home voyage, and indeed Harrison's reckoning proved to be far the more precise. His clock was well within the precision required. However, the Board of Longitude said that because the same captain had not presided over both outward and inward voyages, and because the clock had not been to the West Indies, Harrison could have only £500.

In 1739 Harrison built a smaller and better clock, and in 1749 he produced a third, even more precise than the others. These came to be called H1, H2 and H3. He pressed the Board for further trials, but they prevaricated. Meanwhile he continued improving his machines, and in 1759 produced H4, which proved to be by far the most accurate clock in the

The elegant H4, Harrison's chronometer or 'timekeeper for longitude'.

world, and was small enough to hold in the palm of his hand. He was immensely proud of H4, and said

> Verily I may make bold to say, there is neither any mechanical or mathematical thing in the world that is more beautiful, or curious in texture, than this my watch, or timekeeper for longitude, and I heartily thank almighty God that I have lived so long as to in some measure complete it.

H4 was sent to Jamaica and back, and in four months lost less than two minutes, equivalent to 18 miles, but the Board still refused to pay. Harrison took it to Barbados, and throughout the voyage determined the longitude to within ten miles, but the Board still said he had not

passed the test. He appealed to Parliament, and finally to King George III, who took his side and ordered his government to pay up.

John Harrison finally got his prize money in June 1773, when he was eighty years old, and had been working on the problem for fifty years. He died three years later. However, his skill lived on. A replica of H4 went on Captain Cook's third voyage around the world. Cook didn't survive the trip – he was murdered by a mob on a beach in Hawaii – but the chronometer came back less than a minute wrong after three years at sea! The problem of longitude – a deadly problem for sailors around the world – was solved by a brilliant village carpenter.

John Harrison's four clocks, H1–H4, are on display in the National Maritime Museum at Greenwich.

3. CHARLES BABBAGE'S CALCULATING ENGINES AND ADA LOVELACE'S PROGRAMMES

Charles Babbage was an irascible genius who just failed to build the first ever mechanical computer. Ada Lovelace was his disciple, and possibly the world's first computer programmer.

Charles Babbage was born in Teignmouth in Devon on 26 December 1792. He went to Cambridge with a passion for algebra, and in 1815 moved to London, where he spent most of the rest of his life. He was elected a Fellow of the Royal Society in 1816, only two years after gaining his degree. Twelve years later, he became Lucasian Professor of Mathematics at Cambridge, and reorganised the subject, though he never gave a single lecture himself. He was one of the founders of the Astronomical Society in 1820, and the British Association for the Advancement of Science in 1831.

He applied his talents to all sorts of endeavours. For a time he worked for Isambard Kingdom Brunel, testing the stability and efficiency of the broad gauge railway Brunel was building between Paddington and Bristol. One night Babbage was about to set off along the line when another engine came steaming in the other way; had he left a few minutes earlier the trains would have collided head-on. The other engine was driven by Brunel himself, who had found himself stranded at Swindon in the evening, and had simply commandeered a locomotive to get back to London!

However, what Babbage is remembered for is his calculating engines. He had his grand idea in a Cambridge library while still an undergraduate. He was reading a book of logarithms, and suddenly had the notion that they could be calculated mechanically. Since the abacus, people had used all sorts of devices for helping with calculations, but Babbage's idea was new – he would build a machine that would actually do the sums to calculate the tables. The advantage was that a machine would not make mistakes. Human computers do make mistakes from time to time, and published tables always had errors in them. Babbage's dream was to build a machine to make error-free tables.

The Method of Differences

He decided to design his machine to use the method of differences, which allows complex answers to be calculated simply by adding or subtracting many simple numbers. For example, suppose you wanted to calculate the squares of all the whole numbers; they start off 0x0=0, 1x1=1, 2x2=4, 3x3=9, 4x4=16, 5x5=25. To begin with it's easy, but it gets harder when you want, say, 279×279!

Number	0	1	2	3	4	5	6
Square	0	1	4	9	16	25	36
Difference		1	3	5	7	9	11

Look at the differences between those squares: 1, 3, 5, 7, 9, 11. They are simply the sequence of odd numbers. So to find the next square, that is 7×7, all you have to do is add the next odd number – 13 and 36 make 49. This method of differences is a simple way of finding squares, as long as you can keep adding up accurately – and that is exactly what a machine should be able to do!

The Difference Engine

Because he designed his machine to add or subtract these differences, Babbage called it a Difference Engine. The way it worked was simple. Each cogwheel had ten teeth, and as one turned through, say, six teeth it turned the next one six teeth also. The numbers were added together as the cogwheels turned, and by arranging banks of cogwheels turning in unison he planned the machine to be able to handle long strings of digits.

In 1822 Babbage made a simple six-wheel model difference engine, and it worked! The Royal Society were impressed, and the Astronomical Society gave him their first ever gold medal. Now he had credibility, and he was ready to start on the real thing. This needed serious funding, and he approached the government. He persuaded the Chancellor of the Exchequer to put up £1500, but unfortunately the discussion was vague, and no one took any notes. Babbage seems to have regarded this £1500 as just an advance; the government thought it would cover the entire cost of the machine. However, at least Babbage was able to start making his calculating machine.

He engaged Mr Clement, an engineer who lived in Lambeth, to do the actual machining, and left him to it for four years, while Babbage went off abroad. When he returned and found the money had run out, he applied for more, and, rather surprisingly, got it. In the end the government gave him £17,000, and arranged for fireproof rooms to be constructed in the stable yard of Babbage's house in Bloomsbury.

Unfortunately, Babbage was an unreasonably demanding employer. The precision of the engineering he wanted was almost beyond the technology of the time;

Charles Babbage's original model difference engine (1822).

Mr Clement not only had great difficulty in making the brass cogwheels sufficiently accurate, but was also most unwilling to move his workshop from Lambeth to Bloomsbury. A terrible dispute ensued. All work on the difference engine ceased. The government were annoyed. One critic wrote, 'We got nothing for our £17,000 but Mr. Babbage's grumblings – we should at least have had a clever toy for our money.'

What's more, in the late 1820s, while the argument was still going on, and Babbage was asking for more money, he conceived the idea for an even better machine, the Analytical Engine.

The Analytical Engine

Babbage's analytical engine was to have been far more powerful than the difference engine. It would have done all the work of the difference engine at high speed, but would also have been able to perform a range of much more complex calculations; in fact, it would have been the first programmable computer.

When he conceived the idea for this machine, around 1828, he immediately asked the government for money but, not surprisingly, they refused him any financial backing. He never wrote a detailed account of his plans, and the machine would have remained almost entirely in his mind, but for the assistance of Ada Lovelace.

Why was Babbage so hopeless at finishing things? The difference engine was never finished; the analytical engine was never started, and most of his written works were abandoned in note form. Part of the problem was that he was cantankerous, and spent a lot of his time

complaining. For example, he hated street music. In typically Babbage fashion, he calculated that he'd wasted a quarter of his entire life listening to street musicians. Eventually, after he instigated a campaign, Babbage's Act was passed and buskers were officially banned. However, this made Babbage pretty unpopular. He was booed in the streets. Dead cats were thrown at his house, and when he died on 18 October 1871 few people came to his funeral, and no one cared much.

ADA LOVELACE

Augusta Ada Byron was born on 10 December 1815 in Piccadilly, the only child of that great romantic poet and seducer of women, George Gordon, Lord Byron – 'mad, bad, and dangerous to know'. When she was four months old, her parents divorced very publicly. She never saw her father again, although he wrote about her in *Childe Harold*:

> Is thy face like thy mother's, my fair child
> Ada, sole daughter of my house and of
> my heart?
> When last I saw thy young blue eyes
> they smiled,
> And then we parted – not as now we part,
> But with a hope.

Ada spent most of her life at 10 St James's Square, in the heart of London. She married the future Lord Lovelace in 1835. Her mother was a mathematician – Byron called her the 'Princess of Parallelograms' – and she made sure Ada was trained in mathematics.

In 1833 Ada met Charles Babbage, and was fascinated by his ideas for calculating machines. In a lecture in Turin he proudly

Ada Lovelace: brains, beauty and a disastrous private life.

SKETCH

OF THE

ANALYTICAL ENGINE

INVENTED BY

CHARLES BABBAGE, Esq.

By L. F. MENABREA,

of Turin,

OFFICER OF THE MILITARY ENGINEERS.

WITH NOTES BY THE TRANSLATOR.

[Extracted from the 'SCIENTIFIC MEMOIRS,' vol. iii.]

LONDON:

PRINTED BY RICHARD AND JOHN E. TAYLOR,

RED LION COURT, FLEET STREET.

1843.

The first computer programme? Ada Lovelace's detailed ideas about how a computer might be programmed could easily be missed — the publisher described them merely as 'notes by the translator'.

announced his plans and dreams for the analytical engine. In 1842 this lecture was written up in French by General Menabrea. Ada translated his paper from French into English, and at Babbage's suggestion began to add her own notes about how the analytical engine might be used. In the end her notes were three times as long as the original paper, and they provide the best information we have about the potential of the analytical engine.

Ada's notes explained how Babbage's analytical engine would have taken instructions on punched cards, in what we now call a program. She described the 'store' or memory, and the 'mill' or central processing unit, and she speculated about what the machine might be capable of; it would not produce original ideas, she said, but it would greatly help the advance of science, and it might be helpful in composing music, she thought. She clearly had a vision of the future, and would have loved the computers of today.

Most important of all, she described in detail exactly what instructions the analytical engine would need in order to perform various complex mathematical calculations. We don't know how much of this was her work, and how much Babbage's, since they certainly collaborated, but she was the first person to write it down, and she can therefore reasonably be described as the world's first computer programmer!

Ada had tremendous ambition. She believed she would be able to work out the mathematics of the brain; she may perhaps have heard of George Boole's 1833 vision about the mathematics of the mind, which eventually became his book *The Laws of Thought* (1854), and the foundation of Boolean algebra. She wrote to Babbage: 'The more I study, the more irresistible do I feel my genius to be.' But her life was tragic. She ran up terrible debts, possibly from gambling, but it seems from letters found after her death that she was being blackmailed by John Crosse, with whom she probably had a discreet affair. After she died they found she had even pawned her husband's family jewels. And the world's first computer programmer died from cancer at the age of thirty-six.

The remains of a small demonstration model of the Difference Engine put together by Babbage himself stands in the Science Museum next to a modern construction of the whole beast, glorious in its hundreds of brass cogwheels.

Ada Lovelace's birthplace in Piccadilly has become a delicatessen, but her home at 10 St James's Square, now elegant offices, is marked with a blue plaque.

4. FRANK HORNBY AND MECCANO

Frank Hornby was born in Liverpool on 15 May 1863 at 77 Copperas Hill Road, which is now opposite Lime Street station, and just behind the Adelphi Hotel. He became a book-keeper at a company that imported meat and livestock at 17 James Street. He married Clara Godefroy in 1887, and within three years they had two sons, Roland and Douglas. As the boys began to toddle Frank made toys for them, using his few tools and lots of determination, apparently inspired by Samuel Smiles's book, *Self Help*, which recounts tales of the heroic feats achieved against massive odds by great engineers and industrialists through hard work and dedication.

Gradually, as the boys grew, the toys became more complex; Frank and his sons constructed miniature bridges and trucks from tinplate, but for each new model they had to start from scratch. What Frank wanted was to find a way of changing them – that is, making a variety of toys from one box of materials. He realised he would need parts that were interchangeable, and during a train journey he dreamed up the idea of using perforated strips. He developed the notion, and came up with a half-inch wide strip of metal with a hole every half inch. Combined with small nuts and bolts, thick wire for axles, and simple brass wheels, this made a flexible system suitable for the construction of a vast range of mechanical models.

He patented his idea in 1901, having to borrow the £5 patent fee from his employer, David Elliott. He called the kit

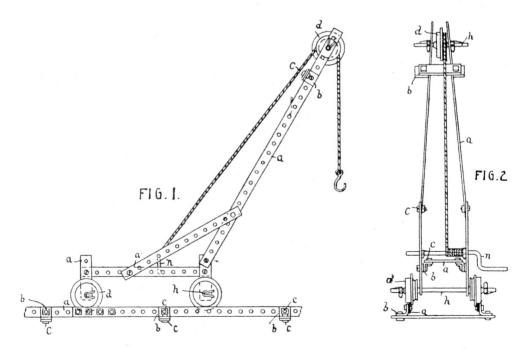

Frank had to borrow £5 to take out his Meccano patent.

Date of Application, 9th Jan., 1901

Complete Specification Left, 9th Oct., 1901—Accepted, 30th Nov., 1901

PROVISIONAL SPECIFICATION.

"Improvements in Toy or Educational Devices for Children and Young People."

I, Frank Hornby of 10, Elmbank Road, Sefton Park, Liverpool in the County of Lancaster, Manager, do hereby declare the nature of this invention to be as follows:—

This invention has for its object a toy or educational device for children.
5 There has been a long felt want among young people for some device which will enable them to construct mechanical objects without the laboriousness of turning, boring, and careful adjustment. The present invention is designed to meet this want, and provide means whereby the interest in mechanical construction from an elementary point of view, is enhanced in addition to pro-
10 viding an interesting means of mechanical education.

It comprises a series of pieces so made that they can be built up and fastened together to form various objects, such as railway lines, railway curves, points, inclines, bridges, tunnels, stations, signals, signal boxes, warehouses, hoists, cranes, pulleys &c, a certain amount of study, ingenuity, or intelligence being
15 required to fit them together, so that the invention while being a toy is also a useful educational device. The pieces are made of metal of various shapes and sizes, such as flat strips of various lengths and widths, angle pieces also of various lengths and widths to form framings, railway sleepers and other structures; rounds pieces or rods to form axles and shafts &c; discs for forming
20 wheels; tubes for forming chimneys, funnels; wires for suspension bridges and so on. The straight pieces are perforated with round holes preferably about half an inch apart each way, and a quarter of an inch or thereabouts from the edges. The angle pieces are also pierced with holes but one set are preferably elongated so as to admit of adjustment. By this
25 means the pieces can be fastened together by bolts and nuts, into a great variety of structures, or screws may be used in which case the holes or some of them are tapped. The discs are perforated in the centre and around the edge to the centre at suitable distances. The wheels or discs have a slot at the centre hole, to admit of their being keyed to a rod or shaft.
30 The flat strips are uniform in thickness. The metal rods are grooved longitudinally to admit of the wheels being keyed on by a child by an arrangement as follows. This comprises a small piece of thin flat steel, bent to grip the shaft. One side of the key is bent and shaped in such a manner as to fit in the groove of the shaft, and at the same time to fit into a slot in the wheel.
35 The other side of the key is straight and prevents the wheel sliding along the shaft when not required to be keyed on to it. In the equipment, a small file may be included so as to cut the metal rods to the desired length, also a screw driver, round nosed pliers to work wire into certain simple designs, and screws and bolts. Cardboard can be employed for the roofs and floors &c of ware-
40 houses, platforms and tunnels and will lend itself to painted designs. By providing various pieces of different shapes provided with a series of holes, they can be so assembled and fastened together that a child of ordinary ingenuity can build a toy railway station, signal boxes, lines, points and other railway

[*Price 8d.*]

Mechanics Made Easy, and sold the first sets for 7s 6d. They contained eighteen pages of instructions explaining how to build twelve models, including the Eiffel Tower and various bridges and cranes. Also included in the first booklet were eight pages of Hornby's introduction to the system. He claimed, 'The aimlessness of an undeveloped fancy will give way to an organised method, and from confused, hazy ideas will spring order and precision.'

A model-building competition was announced in the magazine *Model Engineer* in October 1903 and held in January 1904. The first production factory was opened in 1907 at 10 Duke Street, Liverpool, and Frank changed the name to Meccano. The kits steadily grew as he added gears, pulleys, cranks and clockwork motors. They became increasingly popular, and by 1920 he had more than 1,200 employees. This made Frank a wealthy man and he bought a big house in Maghull, Quarry Brook. In 1920 he introduced Hornby 0-gauge model trains, and in 1934 Dinky toys; in fact, he provided the same sort of enthusiasm and inspiration for young engineers as Arthur Ransome did for young sailors. In 1931 Frank Hornby became MP for Everton.

Frank Hornby died on 21 September 1936, and although children now spend much more time sitting in front of computer and television screens than they do making models, Meccano is still among the best-known and best-loved constructional toys, after almost 100 years.

Frank's grand house at Maghull, Quarry Brook, is now a convent school, but his real memorial is the Meccano that he invented in 1900.

5. Arthur Doodson's Pendulums for Tide Prediction

Arthur Thomas Doodson (1890–1968) was the son of a Lancashire cotton mill manager, and was one of those people who loved not only mathematics but actually performing calculations. In an age before computers, his prodigious ability was used to defend London from Zeppelins, to ensure the perfect timing of the D-Day invasion, and to design and build the best tide-predicting machine in the world.

The port of Liverpool had more interest in the tides than most. Apart from being one of the great ports of the Empire, Liverpool's situation at the end of the fairly shallow Mersey estuary made the pattern of the tides particularly tricky. But the safety and efficient running of the port depended upon being sure when ships could move in or out. So it was not too difficult to persuade

Arthur Doodson setting up the machine used to predict the tides for the D-Day landings.

Liverpool ship owners to pay for a Tidal Institute, which was eventually based at the observatory on Bidston Hill, a magnificent landmark on the Birkenhead side of the harbour entrance. Indeed Bidston Hill was well known to the shipping companies because it was here that a primitive early-warning system was operated in the days before radio made it possible to know precisely where your ships were. On the hill stood a series of flag-poles, and when a ship was spotted heading for the harbour the appropriate company flag was run up the pole so the dock could be made ready. So the Liverpool Tidal Institute was part of a great maritime tradition, and the man they recruited to sort out the calculation and prediction of the tides was Arthur Doodson.

A would-be teacher and keen piano player, Doodson's life changed when he became profoundly deaf. Being mechanically gifted, he made his own hearing aid long before portable hearing aids were generally available, and carried it around in an attaché case. He then thought about being a chemist, but switched to mathematics. He turned out to be particularly good at devising new methods for computing mathematical tables, and his tables were the best yet. He was so keen on computation that he could often be seen calculating away on buses and trams travelling to and from work, and during his lunch hour. In 1916 Doodson's delight in this high-precision but repetitive work singled him out for the ballistics department of the War Office – but here he ran into a problem. He was a deeply religious man – the church seems to have been his main social activity – and a conscientious objector. Apparently he was persuaded that

calculating trajectories for anti-aircraft guns targeting the Zeppelins over London was defensive work, but it must have been uncomfortable for him working in a place dedicated to waging war. Nevertheless, his vision was such that he replaced cruder methods with his own firmly mathematical approach, and ended the war as head of the section. It must have been a relief to move on to the work that dominated the rest of his life – the tides.

At first sight, tides seem quite simple. The water of the oceans is pulled up towards the moon by gravity, forming a 'hump' of deeper water on one side of the globe. There is a corresponding hump on the other side where the water is 'thrown out' by the motions of the earth and moon. As the earth rotates, each place passes under the high and low 'humps' and we experience tides. But the sun also pulls on the water of the oceans, reinforcing (spring tides) or decreasing (neap tides) the effect of the moon, depending upon whether the sun, earth and moon are in line or not. This is just the start of the complexity. If you actually sat in a harbour recording the height of water for a year (as people did), the resulting graph is often very complicated, not least because there are often local effects caused by tidal currents flowing round the land or up shallow estuaries like the Mersey.

So how can you predict the tides for places where you might not even know what the local influences are? Rather than go back to first principles, it was clear that you should start from the actual tides – hence the man recording the height of water for a year. Then a mathematical trick is used. The impossibly complex and apparently irregular tidal curve can be reproduced by adding together several quite regular curves – sine waves. The idea is that if you choose enough regular curves, and get their height and frequency right, you can reproduce any tidal curve, no matter how complex. Then if you run all the regular curves together and add up the results, you should be able to predict the tides into the future.

These principles had been worked out by the 1870s, but Lord Kelvin, charged with reporting to the Tides Committee of the British Association, couldn't work out a neat way of doing the fiendish calculations.

For any major port in the Commonwealth, Doodson's machine can go through the tides for an entire year in just a few hours.

He travelled to the British Association meeting of 1872 by train and found himself in a carriage with Mr Beauchamp Tower, a well-known inventor. Kelvin discussed the problem of adding together many regular movements, all of different sizes and travelling at different speeds. Tower suggested that if you could mechanically represent each regular movement – which is quite easy – then perhaps the sum could be done mechanically as well. He proposed that if the regular movements could be represented by pulley wheels moving up and down, then simply passing a wire over all the pulleys would add up their movements;

if you attached a pen to the end of the wire, it would draw the resulting line. Kelvin realised this was the answer, and presented his solution to the meeting. The machine could add up ten regular tidal 'constituents' and, as he reported, 'the machine may be turned so rapidly as to run off a year's tides for any port in about four hours'.

By the time Doodson became involved with tides in the 1920s, tide-predicting machines had been around for fifty years. But the results were not always very good, especially for unusual ports. Doodson looked very carefully at the tides at Newlyn in Cornwall, and soon devised new methods. It became clear that for good predictions the tides had to be separated into more than forty constituents, each represented in the machine by a moving pulley. The new machines he devised were finally good enough to analyse tides anywhere in the world, and eventually the Liverpool Tidal Institute became responsible for supplying tide predictions for every major port in the Commonwealth.

Arthur Doodson's greatest moment of glory was once again associated with warfare. The government often consulted Doodson as the world's greatest expert in tidal prediction. During the war, it was not unusual for them to supply him with tidal information and ask for a prediction, but concealing where the information came from. The *Express* headline on this occasion was: 'The doctor solves Problem X: Tide wizard's £3000 robot makes its greatest forecast.' Problem X turned out to be calculating the precise tides for the invasion beaches in Normandy on 6 June 1944 – D-Day.

Arthur Doodson's wonderful machine is still on Bidston Hill, but is now run only occasionally.

6. BARNES WALLIS AND THE 'IMPOSSIBLE' BOUNCING BOMBS

I am not generally in favour of war, nor of weapons, but while I was at school in the 1950s my friends and I read avidly about the heroes of the Second World War, which had been going on when we were born, and was still a recent memory for our parents and teachers. Of the books I read then, the one that left the greatest impression on me was Paul Brickhill's *The Dam Busters*, and I was captivated by the ingenuity and the dogged perseverance of its hero, Barnes Wallis.

Barnes Wallis was born in Ripley in Derbyshire on 26 September 1887. His father was a not-very-successful doctor who had suffered from polio, and the family was never well off. However, Barnes was a smart boy, and managed to get a place at Christ's School in the centre of London. It was rather a Dickensian school with wooden beds and a concrete rugby pitch, but the science teacher was way ahead of his time; he believed that science was best taught by experience, rather than by rote learning.

The day before war was declared, according to Brickhill, Wallis abandoned his family on holiday in Dorset and went back to his office at Vickers, where he worked as an aircraft designer. The works stood in the middle of Brooklands – the birthplace of track motor racing, with the first ever banked track – near Weybridge in Surrey.

Wallis wanted to end the war quickly, and reckoned the best way would be to disrupt the industrial heartland of Germany. Coal mines and oil fields were difficult to attack, but he wondered whether it might be possible to blow up some dams. The point of attacking dams was that the Germans needed water to provide hydroelectric power for many factories, and cooling for others. Water was involved in many crucial industrial processes, and water was needed to top up the canals that provided vital transport links. But the particular fact that Wallis latched on to was that the German steel factories needed 8 tons of water to make a ton of steel. Deny them the water, and steel production would grind to a halt; then there would be no tanks, no guns and no ammunition – and no more war.

The author testing bouncing bombs on Silvermere Lake, just as Wallis did.

Wallis dived into the literature, and looked up the specifications of the major dams in the Ruhr Valley – the Möhne, the Eder and the Sorpe. He did some sums and figured out that an ordinary bomb dropped on top of one of these dams would have no chance of demolishing it unless it weighed 30 tons – but this was much more than any existing plane could carry. So he had to find a way of doing the same job with a smaller bomb.

Eventually, after much head-scratching and experimentation, he decided the best chance of success would be to explode a bomb under water against the base of the dam wall. He did some experiments on small-scale models and came to the conclusion that one of these dams could be breached by a correctly placed explosion using only 3 tons of the new explosive RDX. This would mean a bomb weighing only 5 tons, which could just be carried by the new Lancaster bombers.

The question was how to place the bomb against the base of the dam wall. No bomb-aimer could drop a bomb within a couple of feet of the wall from any sensible height; in practice, most bombs fell hundreds of yards from their targets, and Wallis's bomb had to be spot on. The bombs could not be dropped as torpedoes to slice through the water and stick into the walls because the dams were well protected by submarine nets and floating booms.

Then Wallis remembered reading that Nelson claimed to have 'bounced' cannon balls off the water to cause more damage to enemy ships, and he wondered whether bouncing might solve his problem. If the bomb were dropped over the lake, and bounced over the boom and the submarine net to hit the parapet of the dam, it would sink down the wall and would be sure to end up in the right place. But could a 5-ton bomb really bounce on water?

You can skip flat stones across the water by throwing them hard and low with enough spin to keep them level – but bouncing a bomb was a very different matter. Wallis started testing his idea in the garden at his home in Effingham, near Leatherhead in Surrey, by catapulting marbles at a tin bath full of water. The children, back from Dorset, helped note the results and retrieved the marbles from the flower beds.

He moved on to lead balls, which he fired across Silvermere Lake, now in the middle of a golf course; no doubt the mud on the lake-bed is still loaded with lead. His experiments seemed to show that you could bounce anything on water as long as it was travelling fast enough to hit the surface at an angle of less than 8°. He calculated that even 5-ton bombs would bounce if they were dropped from an aircraft flying at 240 mph exactly 60 feet above the water.

The authorities were sceptical; they said he was mad, and laughed at the idea of bouncing bombs – 'quite impossible!' they said. But Wallis was stubborn and persuasive, and eventually convinced them that he could bounce bombs up to the dam walls.

However, a bomb travelling at such a speed might bounce away from the dam wall when it struck. Wallis carried out a long series of tests firing golf balls along the water in one of the huge ship-testing tanks at Teddington, where film shot under water by a brave camerawoman in a glass box showed that the balls behaved better when given backspin.

Backspin may not have been Wallis's own idea; his colleague Farrimond Ogden was an expert on mines, and may have suggested both the use of a cylindrical casing and the principle of backspin for directional stability. In practice, backspin seemed to have three effects. First, because the underside of the missile was spinning forwards, in the direction of travel, the effective speed of impact was increased, which ensured that the missile would bounce even if there were slight waves or other interference – just as with backspin a tennis ball will 'sit up' and bounce higher. Second, if one end of the cylinder hit the water before the other, the bomb would dig in and veer off in that direction; so if the left-hand end hit first, the bomb would turn left, and therefore miss the centre of the dam. With backspin the bomb was stabilised and fell level, so that it set off straight down the lake. Third, when the missile hit the dam and began to sink, the backspin made it hug the dam wall as it fell through the water, so it was bound to be lying against the wall when it reached the bottom.

The bombs were eventually built as steel cylinders, about 5 feet in diameter

The Barnes Wallis bouncing bomb.

and 6 feet long. They were held horizontally across the belly of the aircraft, and spun at up to 500 rpm with an electric motor before being dropped. Fitted with hydrostatic fuses, they exploded not when they hit the dam wall, but when they had sunk 30 feet below the surface of the water.

The bombs had to be dropped from

exactly 60 feet and, as the pilots found, judging this height over water at night was difficult and dangerous. Luckily some bright person came up with the idea of fitting two spotlights below the aircraft, one at each end, so that the spots converged when the aircraft was at the right height. The navigator peered down, watched the spots, and called out 'Down, down, up a bit, steady . . .' and the pilot could keep exactly to 60 feet.

The bombs also had to be dropped at the right distance in front of the dam so they would bounce against the wall and not over it. A bomb-sight expert produced a clever gadget – just a triangle of plywood with a peephole at one corner and a nail standing up on each of the other two corners. The bomb-aimer looked through the peephole at the dam, and released the bomb when the nails lined up with the towers on the dam wall.

The best time to breach the dams was in mid-May, when the water level was at its greatest. Barnes Wallis was given the go-ahead for the bouncing bombs on 26 February 1943; so he had only eight weeks to prepare for the raid. Meanwhile the RAF brought together some of their finest bomber crews to create a new squadron, 617 Squadron, and they started secret training.

On 16 May 1943 nineteen Lancaster bombers took off in the early evening from Scampton in Lincolnshire, and by the light of the full moon headed for the Ruhr Valley. They succeeded in blowing huge holes in two of the target dams, the Möhne and the Eder. Millions of gallons of water poured out. Objectively, the raid was not the strategic triumph that Wallis had hoped for. The dams were repaired fairly quickly, and there was enough water in other reservoirs to sustain most of the German war effort. Meanwhile many civilians and prisoners of war were killed by the floods of escaping water, and eight Lancasters – with fifty-three courageous airmen – failed to return from the raid.

However, the propaganda value of the dams raid was colossal. It did wonders for the morale of the nation at a low point in the war, and the whole country was amazed and delighted at the ingenuity and daring of this extraordinary venture.

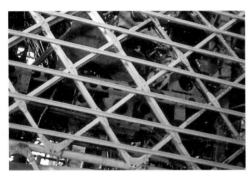

The geodesic structure of Wellington bomber 'R for Robert'.

A stubborn man, and difficult to work with, Barnes Wallis designed many wonderful things, including the legendarily strong spiral fuselage for the R100 airship, later used in the Wellington bomber, and a huge climatic test chamber, used to test equipment at temperatures as low as −65°C, in winds of up to 50 mph, at atmospheric pressures equivalent to an altitude of 70,000 feet. However, he will always be remembered for the dam-busting bouncing bombs.

Silvermere Lake, where Wallis tested his bouncing bomb ideas, is now part of a golf course. Many of Barnes Wallis's inventions, including a bouncing bomb, a 'Grand Slam' bomb, and a Wellington bomber, are on display at the Brooklands Museum, Weybridge (01932 857381).

7. ALASTAIR PILKINGTON'S FLOATING GLASS

Of all the materials that characterise the modern cityscape, glass is surely the most exciting. Breath-taking walls of clear, flat glass are draped over the world's most prestigious buildings, prompting us to wonder how something so solid could be constructed of a material so apparently light and delicate. Perhaps the fixation with vast areas of glass comes from it being a truly modern material: only fifty years ago the process by which most glass is made had not been invented. The man who solved a problem that had challenged technologists since Roman times was Alastair Pilkington – and the answer came to him while he was doing the washing up.

The use of glass in buildings has always been associated with wealth and status – at one time in England there was a window tax. But actually making the stuff flat, clear and in large sheets is a real challenge. Although the Egyptians used it, the Romans first mastered glass – working out how to blow it to make vessels. They discovered that you can't mould glass as you mould clay for pottery because if you touch the surface of molten glass, it loses its transparency. This is why making sheets of flat glass is so difficult – it would be nice if you could simply roll out a piece of glass like making pastry, but that would ruin the surface. So the first successful flat glass process was a development of blown glass, and the 'crown glass' process was used until the middle of the nineteenth century. At first the process looks like blowing a glass bowl. At a critical moment the bowl is put back into the furnace to soften it, and then is withdrawn, spinning fast. The centrifugal force opens the bowl out like a flower, and as the glass-maker keeps spinning it flattens out and stretches until it is perhaps 5 feet in diameter – a smooth sheet of glass with a 'fire finish' that comes from never having touched anything.

Unfortunately, right in the centre of the glass disc is a major fault – the bull's-eye, a nodule where the glass-maker's 'ponty' or iron rod was attached. So the glass is cut into sheets, avoiding the bit in the middle, which was thrown away until it became fashionable to put a bull's-eye into the glass of front doors. Because the disc is circular, rather a lot of the glass round the edge is also wasted. By the time Joseph Paxton came to design the Crystal Palace for the Great Exhibition of 1851, he could rely on a rather more productive process. The cylinder process was also based on glass-blowing and, as its name suggests, involved blowing a huge cylinder of glass, which was allowed to harden before being cut and flattened.

Although machines blowing cylinders a few yards long were eventually produced, this was still very labour intensive and far from a continuous industrial process.

Lionel Alexander Bethune (pronounced Beaton) Pilkington, always known as Alastair, was born in India on 6 January 1920, and educated at Cambridge. The war interrupted his studies quite a bit; he was captured on Crete in 1942 and spent the rest of the war practising his clarinet in a prison camp. He finished his studies when he returned and joined the company which shared his name in 1947. It was with them that he put his mind to making the best flat glass in the world. St Helens was already the centre of the British glass-making industry, largely thanks to the Pilkington factory that had first opened over a century before. It is a curious fact that Alastair was not related to the Pilkingtons who owned the company.

By this time flat glass was made on an industrial scale but they still hadn't got it

Making bigger, better and cheaper glass sheets had been the aim of glassmakers for centuries.

right. Plate glass was made by rolling the glass between metal rollers and then grinding and polishing away the ruined surface that resulted. The end product was good, but the process was hugely wasteful and expensive. More cunning was the 'window glass' process first tried in 1914. The idea was to draw a sticky ribbon of molten glass from the surface of the melted mass in the furnace, rather as you get a long string when you take your spoon out of a jar of treacle. As the ribbon rose, the surface cooled and eventually the glass set. It had the attraction of being continuous, and having an intrinsically good 'fire finish'. But 'window glass' could only be made thin and, worse, the way it cooled led to optical distortions – hence the name: it was all right for domestic windows, but not for anything fancy.

Alastair had joined Pilkingtons to work on the technical side of production, but soon rose into management. He claimed that it was because he was 'bored' that his mind became occupied with the problem of flat glass, and one day in 1952, while he was helping his wife with the washing up, he hit upon the answer. Glass is ruined if during manufacture it touches something solid; but what if the thing it touched was not solid? He realised that it might be possible to float molten glass on molten metal, just as oil floats on water. If you could control everything properly, it might be possible to allow the glass to cool enough to be lifted off the still molten metal as a sheet. Because the liquid metal would be perfectly smooth and flat, so would the glass. It turned out that tin was the metal with the right melting point and so on, but the rest of the process proved to be a bit of a nightmare.

Pilkington's account of how he made the float process work is very different from the way eighteenth and nineteenth-century lone inventors perfected their ideas. The principle of float glass was brilliant: glass would indeed float on tin and could be removed. But he needed a full-scale experimental plant, and had to get exactly right every detail of a process that had never been tried before he could get anything like saleable glass. Every month he would go to the Pilkington board to explain why it was taking so long, and to ask for another £100,000. Having invented the process in 1952, Pilkingtons did not announce it until 1959. In that time Pilkington had to solve chemical problems in the bath, to design spouts to pour glass on to the tin in a particular way, to devise a special atmosphere inside the float chamber, to work out how to cut and handle a continuous ribbon of glass. Most things that could have gone wrong, did, and for most of the development period no useful glass was made.

But they did have one bit of luck. When glass floats on molten tin, it naturally forms a sheet 6 mm thick, which accounts for 50 per cent of the world market in glass! Finally in 1958 they got everything right, announced the process the following year, and then shut down the plant to prepare it for continuous production. When they started up again, the glass was no good and nobody knew why; it took fourteen very expensive months to fix. Today, however, thousands of tonnes of float glass are made every day thanks to the inspiration and perspiration of Alastair Pilkington.

There are now many float-glass factories, but Alastair Pilkington's real memorials are the world's millions of smooth glass windows.

WIND, WEATHER AND SEA

T he weather in this country has always been a subject of endless fascination and small-talk, and yet rather surprisingly the heroes of meteorology are almost unknown. The first person to make systematic measurements of rainfall was Richard Towneley in 1677. Yet he is quite unsung, as is Admiral Sir Francis Beaufort, who, on 28 October 1800, received in a naval engagement three sword cuts and sixteen musket shots in the head, arms and body; he was promoted to Commander for his pains. He survived to be hydrographer to the navy for twenty-six years, and invented the scale of wind-speeds that we still use today:

Beaufort scale	Wind speed (mph)	
1	1–3	Light air
3	8–12	Gentle breeze
5	19–24	Fresh breeze
7	32–38	Moderate gale
9	47–54	Strong gale
11	64–75	Storm

8. WILLIAM BROWNRIGG: POURING OIL ON TROUBLED DERWENTWATER

Derwentwater near Keswick was the site of one of the more bizarre experiments in the history of scientific endeavour. The man who did it wasn't one of the greatest scientists ever, but he took a very serious interest in salt, and showed that oil really does calm troubled waters.

William Brownrigg (1711–1800) was a doctor, living and working mainly in Whitehaven. Despite suggestions that he should move to London, he preferred to stay in the Lake District, tending his patients and studying science. He remains a rather obscure figure in part because he refused to publish much of his work, insisting that he would prefer to wait until it was complete. Brownrigg is rather typical of many eighteenth-century scientists. At that time, science certainly wasn't a full-time profession, so being a doctor or vicar was a useful starting point. Education was a problem, and even provincial doctors had to travel to study – Brownrigg went to the University of Leyden in the Netherlands.

Back in Whitehaven he became interested in problems caused by gases in mines, and arranged to have flammable fire-damp pumped directly into his house for experiments – which sounds rather dangerous. He became a bit of a damp guru, and was apparently able to predict when there would be explosions in mines by the speed of descent of the barometer, and he was often consulted by mine owners. But the work that first brought him to national attention was his treatise on salt. Because Britain was so often at war, supplies of the best salt were often hard to get. Salt was important as a condiment, but also for preserving fish and meat in those days before the fridge. So Brownrigg examined all the ways of producing salt, and suggested that we could make salt every bit as good as that imported at great expense from France, Spain and Portugal.

On the continent, salt was made by using sun and wind to evaporate sea water. British salt, he discovered, was generally made by heating briny water, in the belief that we don't have enough sun. The trouble is that this is very expensive. He also found all sorts of impurities in the salt, including the 'seeds, sperm and excrements of innumerable kinds of plants and animals'. Also, the salt-makers added various things to get the salt to crystallise more quickly – particularly popular was dog fat. Brownrigg said it was quite wrong that we didn't have enough sun in Britain to evaporate sea-water into the finest salt, and there were some experiments in Hampshire to prove it. He showed what sort of saltern (the name for a pond where salt is made) would work best, and that the only modification for the British climate was a removable cover rather like that used on a cricket pitch to keep off the rain, which would otherwise dilute the brine. His treatise, published in the *Philosophical Transactions* of the Royal Society, got him elected a fellow of the Society.

Remember, this was in the days before modern chemistry – Joseph Priestley hadn't really got going – so such a thoroughly scientific approach was very impressive. This work alerted the scientific world to the Cumbrian doctor's existence, and many great scientists made a point of stopping off in the Lakes to see him. But undoubtedly the most amazing incident concerning Brownrigg happened on Lake Derwentwater when, accompanied by a vicar, the President of the Royal Society, and the American scientist and diplomat Benjamin Franklin, Brownrigg investigated the effect of oil on troubled waters. Benjamin Franklin was famous as the man who had proved lightning was electric by flying a kite on the end of a wire during a thunderstorm. To Americans, he is more important as one of the authors of the Declaration of Independence, though he had spent many years as a diplomat trying to avoid revolution.

Like most of us, Franklin had heard the expression 'pouring oil on troubled waters', and Pliny the Elder, the Roman writer, had given an account of it, but Franklin assumed it was all nonsense. But while travelling in a convoy of ships he noticed that the wake of one ship was particularly smooth. Asking why this might be, he was told that the cooks had probably just discharged greasy water through the scuppers. Franklin began to collect other anecdotes. Bermudans used oil to calm the water above fish they hoped to spear if the surface was ruffled. Fishermen of Lisbon supposedly used oil to suppress the breakers as they returned to harbour. Portuguese clam divers would actually dive down with their mouth full of olive oil, and release some to calm the surface above, giving them a clearer view of the sea-bed, presumably because the light illuminating the bottom normally passes through waves, resulting in confusing patterns. There were yet more stories: harbours in northern regions were supposed to be very calm when blubbery

The author on Lake Derwentwater looking for still water, having tipped in a teaspoon of olive oil, following Brownrigg's method.

whales were brought in, and the sea over oily fish like mackerel is said to be still.

Franklin determined to try this himself, and first did so on the pond at Clapham Common in London, where he happened to be. The effect of just a little oil was so striking that from then on he kept some oil in the hollow handle of his walking cane in case the opportunity arose to try it again. In 1772 Franklin travelled north with Sir John Pringle, President of the Royal Society, and they dropped in on Brownrigg. The three men, together with the Revd Farish of Carlisle, set out to pour oil on to Derwentwater. We know about this from a letter Franklin wrote to Brownrigg the following year, summarising his investigations. Franklin noticed the dramatic spreading of even a little oil, forming a film so thin it produces what he called 'prismatic colours'. We now know that some oil films are just one molecule thick, and that the colours result when the thickness of the film is similar to the wavelength of light, so that certain colours in the reflected light from the water interfere with those in the reflection from the film of oil.

Strangely, neither in Franklin's letter to Brownrigg nor anywhere else does he record exactly what took place that day. However, Franklin describes what generally happens. Clearly the oil does have an effect – at least on the tiniest wind ripples. Franklin then speculated that the oil prevents the wind 'getting a grip' on the water, and this not only prevents tiny ripples, but stops the wind making existing waves bigger. Actually, there are a couple of modern explanations. It may be to do with surface tension trying to keep the oil film flat, but there is also a more surprising explanation. When waves form on water, the surface of the wavy water must be larger than that of flat water. But if the oil film is just one molecule thick, it *cannot* stretch over the waves without breaking. The force holding the film together is enough to flatten the waves. But whatever the reason, the mythical 'pouring oil on troubled waters' really does work. It is wonderful to think of a Cumbrian doctor, the President of the Royal Society, one of the greatest Americans of all time and a vicar all taking time to pour oil on to a lake.

Brownrigg remained in the lakes, refusing to be tempted by London scientific society. As a result, no one much has heard of him. A nice tribute was paid by the president of the Royal Society, who called him 'my very learned, very penetrating, very industrious but too modest friend, Dr Brownrigg'.

Brownrigg's home is a private house, but Derwentwater is still sometimes troubled.

9. GEORGE MANBY AND HENRY TRENGROUSE: MORTARS AND ROCKETS

The parallels between these two life-saving men of the sea are quite striking. They were contemporaries, Manby from East Anglia, Trengrouse from Cornwall. Both were moved by seeing a tragic accident in which they were helpless to prevent many lives being lost. Both struggled to overcome the same technical problems. And although between them they saved many hundreds of lives, both failed to get the credit they deserved.

George William Manby (1765–1854) lived much of his life in the shadow of England's greatest maritime hero, Horatio Nelson, who had attended the same school as Manby in Downham Market, Norfolk. Manby claimed great intimacy with Nelson, but the dates don't quite add up – Manby was only five years old when Nelson, aged twelve, went off to sea, so in fact they can scarcely have known one another.

Although Manby spent most of his working life as a soldier, he was also an author, and he turned to literature when unspecified 'domestic troubles' caused him and his new wife to leave Denver in Norfolk, where he had been born, and move abruptly to Bristol. Most of his writing consisted of travel guides, but in 1803 he wrote a pamphlet entitled 'An Englishman's Reflexions on the Author of the Present Disturbances', in which he discussed the threatened invasion of England by Napoleon. This work attracted the notice of Charles Yorke, then Secretary at War, and in August 1803 Manby was appointed barrack-master at

Yarmouth. It was there that Manby witnessed the dramatic and horrifying spectacle that was to change his life.

In February 1807 there was a great storm off the east coast, and a gun brig, the *Snipe*, went aground off Yarmouth. As usual word soon went around that a ship was wrecked, and people rushed to the spot. The *Snipe* was just 60 yards off shore, and was being smashed to pieces by the fierce wind and waves driving in from the east. Her passenger list included French prisoners of war, and many women and children. Although some escaped, sixty-seven people, including the captain, were drowned. All this happened within sight of Manby and the crowd on shore – but they were quite unable to do anything

about it. Altogether that day a further 147 bodies were picked up along the coast. You can imagine Manby's horror, made worse by the feeling of impotence at having been so near and so unable to help. Incredibly, this was a far from uncommon incident. Manby resolved to make sure it couldn't happen again.

It is easy to see how disaster could strike a ship going aground in some remote location, but less easy to see why the *Snipe* and unfortunate vessels like it should be doomed to disaster so close to people who should have been able to help. The answer lies in the nature of ships and of storms. Sailing ships use their sails in two ways, like parachutes when 'running' with the wind behind them, or like wings to provide

The Manby mortar in action and doing what it was meant to do: hurling a line into the teeth of a howling gale, where no rescue ship could go.

lift when the wind is in front. But the wing works only when it makes an angle with the wind, and so no ship can sail directly into the wind – it has to 'tack' back and forth at an angle to the wind to get the best out of its sails. So if a ship is driven on to rocks by an on-shore gale – where the wind blows from the sea directly on to the shore – it is truly helpless and thus doomed.

The ship cannot sail off again, because that would mean sailing directly into the wind – which is impossible. Worse, no would-be rescuers can sail in behind the wrecked ship, since they would be certain to end up the same way. The same problem affected the people on land: it was impossible to get a line out to the ship as this would mean throwing it into the teeth of the gale. Which is how sixty-seven lives came to be lost within 60 yards of the shore.

Manby's invention was inspired by a boyhood prank in which he had fired a rope over the roof of the church at Downham. He got hold of a mortar, essentially a small stubby cannon, and started experimenting. The mortar fired an iron ball about 2½ inches in diameter, to which a rope was attached; it had to be able to travel, with its rope, at least a couple of hundred yards if it was to do any good. The kick to do this came from the gunpowder charge in the mortar, and was so violent and explosive that the rope often broke or was burned. Manby tried using a chain between ball and rope, but the chain snapped. Eventually he settled on a leather strap attached to the ball, which absorbed some of the shock and didn't burn. He demonstrated his invention to the Suffolk Humane Society in the autumn of 1807. The first real trial came on 12 February 1808, when it was used successfully at the wreck of the brig

Elizabeth. Soon after this, mortar kits, designed to be quickly carried to the scene of a disaster, were issued to coastguard stations up and down the country, with 302 sets eventually in place. Manby was awarded the very substantial sum of £2000 – pretty generous at a time when the price of a pint of beer was tuppence.

Manby's system is credited with saving hundreds of lives, and you might have thought he would have died happy. Following the mortar, he invented numerous other life-saving devices including the fire-extinguisher, a lifeboat, a jumping-sheet (for catching people leaping from burning buildings) and a device for rescuing people who had fallen through ice. All these were described in pamphlets published by Manby himself, but none met with the success of the mortar. Meanwhile, Manby's private life took a turn for the worse. He got into a fight with his wife's lover, which resulted in his being shot in the back of the head. He recovered, following an operation to remove from his skull the bullets and bits of his hat, and he

Presumably this portrait of George William Manby was done before he suffered gunshot wounds to the back of his head, following an argument with his wife's lover.

carried these grisly souvenirs with him in a small box for the rest of his life. Despite the money and acclaim, Manby ended his life in service to Nelson; he ran and lived in a museum dedicated to him at Yarmouth.

Manby's device was not, however, the final solution to the onshore-gale problem. At about the time Manby was demonstrating his mortar, Henry Trengrouse, a cabinet maker from Helston in Cornwall, witnessed a shipwreck in chillingly similar circumstances. The frigate HMS *Anson* had left Falmouth on 28 December 1807, heading to her station at Brest when a storm struck. She was driven toward the breakers at Lizard Point. Captain Lydiard tried to run her on to the sand at Loe Bar, a few miles along the coast. She ran aground 60 yards from shore but, luckily, heeled landwards and the masts formed a sort of bridge to the beach. Many lucky sailors scrambled through the waves to safety but more than 100 people, including Captain Lydiard, were drowned.

Like Manby, Trengrouse was standing on the shore watching helplessly, and he too vowed to invent a system to prevent this type of disaster happening again. He tried unsinkable boats, but it was the celebration of the king's birthday that provided the answer. Part of the festivities on Helston Green included a firework display, and Trengrouse wondered if a rocket-powered line might be the answer.

This sounds just like Manby's idea – but there was one crucial difference. Trengrouse planned to put his lightweight rockets on to the ships, so that grounded ships could help themselves rather than depending upon running aground near a spot with a mortar. The rockets had several advantages: they accelerated gradually, eliminating the problem of the snapping line; in an onshore gale they would be carried by the wind to the shore; and as a target you had only to hit the shore, whereas mortar crews had to aim for the ship. News of Henry's rocket device travelled as far as Russia,

The wreck of HMS *Anson*, witnessed by Trengrouse. Although the picture shows passengers and crew being hauled off, over 100 people died within yards of the shore, convincing Trengrouse that a way must be found to prevent such a tragedy happening again.

where Alexander I was so impressed he wrote to Henry and gave him a diamond ring. The Russian ambassador asked him to come to St Petersburg to continue development of the rocket, but he remained loyal to king and country. Unfortunately, king and country ignored his idea.

The Admiralty finally ordered twenty rockets, for which they paid him £50, but then ripped him off – they made the rockets themselves without paying him any royalty at all.

Ironically, although the mortar was much more popular in the 1800s, it is the rocket that has stood the test of time. Lightweight versions are still carried on lifeboats today and must have saved thousands of lives. Henry Trengrouse died and is buried in Helston where he spent his whole life – an unsung hero if ever there was one.

A plaque commemorates the loss of the Anson *by the beach at Loe Bar. The RNLI carry life-saving rockets on every lifeboat.*

Trengrouse's splendid memorial, remembering his rocket apparatus.

10. RICHARD TOWNELEY, RECORDER OF RAINFALL

Occasionally the weather forecasters on radio and television say things like 'last month was the wettest since records began'. One day I wrote to Bill Giles and asked him when records did begin, and the helpful reply told me that the first systematic recording of rainfall in Britain began in 1677, and the man who did it was Richard Towneley.

Richard Towneley was born in 1629. His father Charles was killed at the Battle of Marston Moor in 1644. As Catholics, the family suffered a good deal of persecution during the turbulent seventeenth century. Towneley Hall, south-east of Burnley in Lancashire, had been home to the Towneley family since the early thirteenth century. Oliver Cromwell took the house away, but by 1653 Richard had got it back again, and began practising science. He was interested in all sorts of things, but especially meteorology – the air, the wind and the rain.

In 1676 he made a rain gauge, which he described in detail to the Royal Society. He took a 'round tunnel' – presumably he means a cylinder – of 12 inches in diameter, and soldered it to a lead pipe. He wanted to make sure that no nearby building could interrupt the falling rain, so he fixed the cylinder on the roof, and took the pipe down and in through his bedroom window. Nowadays the Meteorological Office advise you not to put a rain gauge on the roof, because wind eddies can sweep rain over the top and give false readings. But Towneley didn't know about that.

In his bedroom he let the water collect in a bottle, to show how much rain had fallen. He measured it three times a day for more

Towneley Hall, captured by Cromwell but eventually returned to the Towneley family — to become a centre for scientific enquiry and the site of the first regular recording of rainfall.

than twenty-five years, and faithfully recorded his results. In 1689 he reported the first ten years' observations to the Royal Society, and his first conclusion was that twice as much rain fell on Towneley as on Paris. He said he thought this was because of the high ground in Yorkshire and east Lancashire; the prevailing south-west winds bring in the rain clouds which 'are oftener stopt and broken and fall upon us'. So if you are thinking of going on holiday to look for the sun, then on Towneley's evidence Paris might possibly be a better bet!

Towneley also used to record the behaviour of the wind, and measured the air pressure with a barometer. He recorded his lowest ever reading of 28.47 inches of mercury in the evening of 26 November 1703. That night England was battered by the worst storm in recorded history – the storm that carried away the first Eddystone lighthouse, along with its builder, Henry Winstanley.

Being a politically non-correct Catholic Towneley never went to London to join the Royal Society. Instead he stayed in Lancashire and enjoyed inviting other philosophers to visit him. The brilliant John Flamsteed dropped in just before he became the King's Astronomer, and they became friends. When Flamsteed went to Greenwich, he wanted a super-accurate clock that would run for a whole year so that he could find out whether the earth's rotation was regular. Richard Towneley made the escapement mechanism for this clock.

Pendle Hill, 1,830 feet high and only 10 miles from Towneley Hall, stands in the middle of Pendle Forest, famous for the 'witches of Pendle', who came from two rival families there. They were accused of witchcraft on the unsupported testimonies of a nine-year-old girl from one of the families, a senile woman, and a half-witted labourer; one died in prison but ten were found guilty at the Assizes, and were hanged on 20 August 1612.

Richard Towneley climbed up Pendle Hill with his friend Henry Power on 27 April 1661. They carried a long tube and a bottle of mercury to test what became known as Towneley's hypothesis. He was interested in the 'spring of the air', and believed that if you had a fixed amount of air – as in a balloon – then the pressure and the volume were related; the higher the pressure, the smaller the volume, and vice versa.

So he collected some 'Valley Ayr', and took it a thousand feet up Pendle Hill, and showed that its volume increased – because the pressure at the top of the hill is less than the pressure at the bottom. Likewise he showed that if he collected 'Mountain Ayr' and took it down, then its volume decreased. And he discovered that multiplying together the volume and the pressure always gave the same answer. In other words, the pressure and volume of a fixed mass of air are inversely proportional to one another.

Other people had taken barometers up mountains before, but this relationship was a new idea. Robert Boyle picked it up, investigated it further, and wrote about it in 1663, and ever since then most people have called the relationship Boyle's Law, but at the time Isaac Newton, Robert Hooke and Robert Boyle himself called it Mr Towneley's Hypothesis.

Towneley Hall, a few miles south-east of Burnley, is open to the public and stands in a lovely park, which includes a golf course. Pendle Hill, north-west of Burnley, offers a good stiff climb with a commanding view from the summit; on a clear day you can see Blackpool Tower and North Wales.

11. ROBERT FITZROY, INVENTOR OF THE WEATHER FORECAST

Most of us take the weather forecast for granted. It appears daily in the papers, hourly on the news, and on television it has its own cable channel. For most of us, predictions of tomorrow's weather are of mainly academic importance, but for farmers, pilots and fishermen, knowing the weather in advance is crucial. The first person to attempt systematic weather forecasting was Robert Fitzroy. He was a naval man, a brave and gallant sea-captain and a brilliant sailor but, as Charles Darwin discovered, he was a difficult man to live with, and he came to a tragic end.

Robert Fitzroy was born at Ampton Hall, a few miles north of Bury St Edmunds in Suffolk, on 5 July 1805 – three months before the battle of Trafalgar. He was the second son of the second son of the 3rd Duke of Grafton, and his mother died when he was five years old, so he probably had rather a tough and disciplinarian childhood. He went to naval college, and then to sea, and when he was only twenty-three the captain of his survey ship died, and Fitzroy was appointed to take command. The ship was the *Beagle*.

For her second voyage to South America in 1831 he decided he should take along a companion – some well-bred gentleman to share his day-cabin and to dine with. After much thought, he decided the right sort of person would be a scientist, who should bring on board culture and interesting conversation.

The *Beagle* was only 90 feet long and 24 feet wide, but carried a total crew of

Five years on the *Beagle* with the difficult Fitzroy must have been a challenge for Charles Darwin.

seventy-four, including a carpenter, a blacksmith, and a missionary. After a curious selection process Fitzroy offered the post of ship's naturalist to a young man called Charles Darwin, who jumped at the chance, even though his father objected at first, and the cabin was so small he could not stand upright in it. Neither of them knew the voyage would last five years, nor that Darwin would as a result of it write his wildly controversial book *On the Origin of Species*.

Fitzroy was neurotic and irascible, and sharing a cabin with him for five years must have been a considerable ordeal. Nevertheless, the voyage was a major success. When they returned, Fitzroy wrote an account of the voyage in two volumes; Darwin wrote a third volume which came to be called *The Voyage of the Beagle*.

In 1843 Fitzroy became Governor of New Zealand, but left under a cloud a couple of years later, and returned to England. His difficult character stood in the way of his landing a senior naval or diplomatic post, which is probably why in 1854 he took up the curious position of Head of the Meteorological Department of the Board of Trade. He was determined to make a success of the job, and a name for himself, and in 1861 he invented the weather forecast.

First he asked ships' captains, once they reached port, to post him details of the weather they had encountered. Then he saw the potential of the new electric telegraph, which would allow him to gather information much more rapidly and reliably. In order to ensure it was accurate and consistent, he set up twenty-four observing stations around the country, and issued each with a standard barometer and instructions on how to use it. Each day he compiled a summary in the form of a synoptic chart or weather map.

Every year in the early 1850s about a thousand ships were wrecked and some thousand lives lost near the British coast. At three in the morning on 26 October 1859 the sailing ship *Royal Charter* sank in a gale off Anglesey, with the loss of 400 lives and half a million pounds' worth of gold bullion. Fitzroy wrote a report about the disaster, and pointed out in words of one syllable that the storm could have been predicted at least twelve hours in advance using the information he had gathered. If the captain had been warned, he could have avoided the storm and saved the ship.

Fitzroy was therefore encouraged to issue storm warnings, and he invented a simple display system. A solid black cone point downwards – a 'south cone' – warned that a southerly gale was imminent; a 'north cone' – point up – warned of a northerly gale. These cones were used in every port, and provided useful warnings to sailors for more than a hundred years.

Encouraged by the success of his storm warnings, Fitzroy went further, and in August 1861 began to predict the weather. People knew a good deal about weather – for example, Cristoph Buys Ballot's Law said that if you stand with your back to the wind in the northern hemisphere then atmospheric pressure is lower on your left than on your right; and many 'experts' were happy to predict what they thought would happen locally the next day, but no one before Fitzroy had seriously tried to forecast the weather for the whole country. From 1862 his weather forecasts were printed in *The Times*.

Fitzroy barometers, like this one from Sheringham, were provided to help fishermen predict the weather.

They aroused considerable interest. The British have always been fascinated by weather, and when people saw forecasts in *The Times* they were amazed and delighted – except that the forecasts were often wrong. Today we are used to inaccurate weather forecasting. We know that even with the help of vast computers the meteorologists cannot be perfect, since the great engine of the atmosphere is too complex to be described by the models the forecasters use. Mathematical chaos ensures that the minutiae of meteorology will always be unpredictable.

However, in Fitzroy's day, people did not understand this, and he became the butt of terrible complaints and jokes. In 1864 questions about his forecasts were asked in the House of Commons. Even *The Times* said 'we must . . . demand to be held free of any responsibility for the too-common failures which attend these prognostications. During the last week Nature seems to have taken special pleasure in confounding the conjectures of science.'

As a fundamentalist Christian, Fitzroy had been seriously offended when Darwin's *Origin of Species* was published in 1859, since it seemed to suggest that God had not designed all creatures great and small – and it was all because he, Fitzroy, had taken Darwin on the *Beagle*. Now the most important people in the country, far from being impressed by his skill and ingenuity in predicting the weather, were pouring scorn on his incompetence. On 30 April 1865, Admiral Robert Fitzroy took his razor, cut his own throat, and died.

Fitzroy barometers are still preserved in a few maritime museums around the country.

12. THOMAS ROMNEY ROBINSON'S CUP ANEMOMETER

Armagh Observatory was built in 1790. Its director for almost sixty years, from 1823 to 1882, was a man of exceptional versatility and vitality, even among my heroes. He made significant contributions to astronomy, meteorology, electricity, magnetism, turbines, air-pumps, fog signals and balloons. He even stressed to ladies the importance of chemistry! In an address to the Royal Irish Academy in 1852 he said 'The person who cultivates only one branch of science cripples his

mind, and does himself an injustice.' His name was Thomas Romney Robinson.

Thomas Romney Robinson was born in Dublin on 23 April 1792. He was a child prodigy, reading avidly by the time he was three, and having a book of poems published when he was only thirteen. He became rector of Enniskillen, and then director of Armagh Observatory when he was thirty-one.

The most worthy thing he did was to compile a catalogue of the positions of 5,345 stars – a huge task involving ten years of solid work for him and his assistant Neil McNeil Edmondson. When it was published in 1859 it won him the Royal Medal of the Royal Society, and he said proudly 'Already it has taken its place among the standard catalogues of reference'. But Mr Edmondson said, 'The fact is, Doctor, it has made old men of us.'

In 1849 Robinson read a paper in Belfast about his observations of the moon. He made a number of statements which show the depth of his understanding:

We see only one side of the Moon, because it turns on its axis at the same rate as it revolves about the Earth; so the same side always faces us.

It has no atmosphere, because stars going behind it disappear suddenly, whereas if there were any atmosphere they would go slowly.

Things on the Moon's surface are light and spongy. A body weighing 6 lb on Earth would weigh only 1 lb on the Moon.

From the length of the shadows we know there are cliffs on the Moon 25,000 feet high, while on Earth there are none more than 500 feet.

The official picture of Armagh Observatory doesn't do full justice to Robinson's anemometer — it is just visible to the left of the right-hand dome.

He was always interested in anything that might upset his astronomical observations. Railways, for example: they shook telescopes and, by using his influence in the House of Lords, he managed to prevent people from building railways not only at Armagh, but also at Greenwich and Oxford.

Wind also rocked the telescope. What was the best way to measure wind speed? After much thought and consideration of various types of apparatus then in use, he invented the cup anemometer. He reckoned that hemispheres would be efficient and easy to reproduce – anyone could make them. He experimented, and decided that four arms were better than three or five. He calculated that if there were no friction, the speed of the cups would be exactly one-third of the wind speed, which turned out to be correct. And finally this elegant machine does not

have to be turned round to face the wind. It works just as well wherever the wind comes from.

This was such a good piece of design that no one has bettered it yet. You've probably seen them in airports; meteorologists all over the world use cup anemometers, although they often make them with three arms.

Rockets for Longitude

But what really endears Robinson to us was the way he set out to find out where he was. At the 1834 meeting of the British Association for the Advancement of Science in Edinburgh, and at the 1838 meeting in Newcastle, he and others agreed to measure very accurately the longitudes of Cambridge, Oxford, Dublin and Armagh, basically to check the maps. We now assume our maps are absolutely accurate, but 150 years ago there was some uncertainty about the exact positions of places. So they wanted to measure their longitude, and they proposed to do it by two different methods.

They persuaded the famous clockmaker Mr E.J. Dent to visit them with fifteen chronometers. These were all synchronised at Greenwich, then Mr Dent carried them in a wooden box on his knee for 500 miles by train in England, 275 miles at sea by steamship, and 190 miles by stage-coach in Ireland. The whole journey took only a week, being performed, as Robinson remarked, 'with the marvellous rapidity of modern improvement'.

But Robinson also wanted to use direct observation, so his second method was to set up a signal that could be seen from both Armagh and Dublin simultaneously. Then they could be sure their clocks were exactly synchronised. There isn't a mountain high enough to be visible from both places, but the highest mountain between Armagh and Dublin is Slieve Gullion, and from Slieve Gullion they could fire rockets high enough for the explosions to be visible from both 18 miles away in Armagh and 51 miles away in Dublin.

Robinson sent his son up the mountain to organise the rockets, with assistance from Lieutenant Thomas Larcom of the Ordnance Survey, who provided them with maps, tents and, most important, rockets. They set up camp on the mountain on 13 May 1839. The Rector of Forkhill provided remarkable hospitality, even for Ireland, including food and two policemen in case of trouble. But the only trouble came from the weather; it snowed, and for two nights that week they couldn't fire any rockets.

Robinson sat in the observatory in Armagh; his friend William Rowan Hamilton sat in Dublin, and they both had to measure as accurately as possible the time of the rocket bursts. Robinson also trained three assistants by getting them to write down the times of shots from a flintlock pistol. Robinson sat in the dark by his telescope, and every now and then looked at the precise grandfather clock by the light of a candle, and he counted the seconds in his mind. 'Five past one, and 10 seconds, 11 . . . 12 . . . 13 . . . 14 FLASH – there it goes – 14.4 seconds – write it down.'

They started firing the rockets at 10 o'clock at night, since they could see the signal better in the dark. They fired fifteen rockets the first night, at five-minute intervals, thirteen the next night, and more at the end of the week. Each rocket provided one precise observation in Armagh and another in Dublin. Robinson and Hamilton both knew their own local time accurately, by observations. After watching the rocket explosions they could synchronise their clocks, and measure precisely the difference between local time in Dublin and local time in Armagh.

The result of this heroic set of experiments was completely to revise the difference in longitude between Dublin and Armagh from 1 minute 14.220 seconds to 1 minute 14.258 seconds. In other words, by letting off several pounds of high explosive into the night sky, Thomas Romney Robinson showed that Armagh was further west of Dublin than anyone had suspected by a distance of nearly 2 feet!

Armagh Observatory is a fine building with an original Robinson anemometer mounted on a tower; note how far west it is!

13. LEWIS FRY RICHARDSON, BULLETS AND PARSNIPS

Lewis Fry Richardson was the first person to develop serious mathematical methods of weather modelling and prediction. A creative and painstaking experimentalist and a brilliant mathematician with the courage to tackle problems of daunting complexity, he worked not only in meteorology but also on the mathematics of war, seismology, electromagnetism and the psychology of perception. He even produced early insights into the mathematics of fractals and chaos, which became fashionable only in the 1980s.

He was born in Newcastle on 11 October 1881, the youngest of seven children, and at an early age showed promising experimental ingenuity. When he was five, his shrewd sister told him that 'money grows in banks'; so he planted some money in a bank in the garden, but it didn't grow; he reckoned his sister's hypothesis was wrong!

After going to schools in York and Newcastle he studied physics at Cambridge, where one of his teachers was J.J. Thompson, before working in a number of research posts at the National Physical Laboratory, at Aberystwyth, Gateshead, Manchester, Eskdalemuir and Paisley. A loner by nature, he seems to have shunned the major academic institutions, partly perhaps as a result of the reaction to his first scientific paper. Tackling the problem of how to cut drainage channels in peat, he found that correct equations existed, but were fiercely complex, required great mathematical skill, and worked only if the peat was in nice circles to start with.

What he needed was a rough-and-ready method to get an approximate answer.

Richardson's clever and simplifying approximations gave him the answers he needed, but failed to impress the referees of *Philosophical Transactions*, who stood in the way of his paper for months, and his dissertation so baffled the fellows of King's College Cambridge that they appealed to the mathematicians of Trinity, who said this approximate stuff just wasn't proper mathematics. So Richardson never went back to Cambridge.

On holiday on the Isle of Wight, he met Dorothy Garnett, sister of his colleague Stuart; they were married in 1909. They were on holiday again in 1912 when he heard about the disaster of the *Titanic*'s collision with an iceberg. Richardson immediately tried experiments to detect large obstacles at sea using the echoes from a beam of sound. He focused the sound with an umbrella – he called it a searchsound – and chose to use the high frequency of a whistle so that even sloping surfaces would be rough compared with the wavelength of the sound waves and would therefore reflect them back. He and Dorothy sat in a small boat, blowing sharp blasts on the whistle, focusing them with the umbrella, and using a watch to measure how long the echoes took to return from the pier. With these crude experiments Richardson showed that sound echoes could provide an effective way of detecting and locating objects over the sea. His invention was the precursor of sonar.

In the bleak and humid solitude of Eskdalemuir he finished the first draft of his book about numerical weather prediction. He lost the manuscript while he was driving an ambulance in France in April 1917, but luckily found it a few months later under a heap of coal! It was eventually published in 1922, and he said in it how he reckoned that to 'race the weather for the whole globe' would take 64,000 human computers armed with slide rules in a vast hall. He reckoned he could predict the weather for the following day working on his own, but the calculations would take three months!

His dream was to set up hundreds of recording stations throughout Europe to measure the conditions in the atmosphere: temperature, pressure, humidity and wind speed. He devised a cunning (although rather bizarre) method of measuring the speed and direction of the wind. Out in the country he built a corrugated-iron shed with a hole in the middle of the roof. Then he took a gun and fired a spherical bullet vertically upwards through the hole. If there were no wind at all, the bullet should fall back down the barrel of the gun, but any wind would blow it sideways. By observing exactly where the bullet fell, and knowing its mass and size, he could calculate the speed and direction of the wind.

Before he fired the gun Richardson and his assistant would put on hard hats and then call out a warning: 'DANGER, DANGER, WARNING – BULLETS MAY FALL, KEEP OFF!' Then they would fire the gun and carefully observe the fall of the bullet. He packed his own cartridges, so he was able to use three different sizes of bullet and also to vary the amount of gunpowder. This meant he could fire bullets to any height he wanted, so if the wind was blowing in one direction near the ground but in a different direction

'Danger, Danger, Warning: Bullets may fall. Keep off!' Richardson's cunning but dangerous method of firing bullets to measure the wind speed. Note the tin hut to protect the weather men.

higher up, he could measure both wind velocities separately.

His use of a gun was slightly surprising, since he was born and raised a Quaker, and was a pacifist, strongly opposed to war. But his best-known mathematical speculation was about human confrontation. He saw an analogy between meteorology and human conflict: molecules are like individual people, and the atmosphere is like the global population. He was prompted to model the causes of war with the aim of preventing them.

In 1919 he wrote a fifty-page essay on the mathematical psychology of war, suggesting that variables such as the animosity of each side could be measured and given a numerical value, and he wrote:

To have to translate one's verbal statements into mathematical formulae compels one carefully to scrutinise the ideas therein expressed. Next the possession of formulae makes it much easier to deduce the consequences. In this way absurd implications, which might have passed unnoticed in a verbal statement, are brought clearly into view and stimulate one to amend the formula.

He published the essay himself; 300 copies cost him £35.

Later on he began to develop mathematical psychology by devising numerical measurements of sensations – perception of touch, colours, sound, thoughts and pain. This was fantastically complicated, and he showed considerable courage and skill in attempting to get to grips with such nebulous ideas. He devised what is now called the 'semantic differential' to give some measure of position on an abstract scale. For example, the publishers might want to know whether this book is boring or fascinating. This is difficult to measure directly, but if they were to ask readers to give the book a number between 1 and 5, where 1 means very boring, 2 means dull, 3 means ok, 4 means interesting, and 5 means 'I could not put it down', then readers would easily be able to give the book a score.

On Holy Loch in 1948 Richardson and his friend Henry Stommel conducted a wonderful experiment with parsnips. Richardson wanted to find a way of describing mathematically the turbulence in a sea-loch. His equations showed him that if he could pick two points close together in the water and then see how the distance between them changed with time he could measure how turbulent the flow was. In order to follow two points in the water he needed some objects that would float low in the water so that they would be influenced by the current rather than the wind, light-coloured so that he could easily see them in dark water, and cheap. After some experiments he discovered that parsnips were perfect, since they are cheap, white and almost as dense as water. He cut them into slices, and weighted each slice with a nail so that it just showed above the surface. He threw two slices together into the loch, and measured their separation every 15 seconds until they had drifted too far away. Then he threw in another pair, and repeated the process. This parsnip experiment was typical of the man: using simple, crude techniques he was able to attack enormously complex mathematical problems.

He also designed, in 1949, a wind-stress experiment, to measure the horizontal force of wind on young turnips. His plan was to plant turnips in a box on a steel table, dig a big hole in the middle of a field of turnips, and suspend the table by its legs in the hole so that the top was level with the surface. Then an observer sitting underground in a second hole alongside would use a microscope to observe the sideways shift of the table when the wind blew, and so be able to calculate the force on the turnips. Alas, this experiment was never carried out, and we may never know how much wind-stress young turnips suffer.

Meteorologists today still use Richardson's 4/3 Diffusion Laws, and Richardson's Number, a measure of whether atmospheric turbulence is likely to increase, and there is a Richardson Building at the Meteorological Office.

14. JOHN TYNDALL'S BLUE SKY

Although Tyndall's story is fairly extraordinary, he might have remained a competent but obscure physicist but for his charm and amazing ability to communicate scientific ideas to any audience. The impact he made on the public resulted in him getting to the very top of his profession, succeeding Michael Faraday at the Royal Institution – and working out why the sky is blue.

John Tyndall was born in Leighlinbridge, County Carlow, on 2 August 1820. Although the family owned a little land, they were quite poor and only the 'superior intellect' of John's father (also John) made sure that young John received a decent education at the nearby National School. He took an immediate interest in mathematics and obtained a job with the Ordnance Survey of Ireland, followed by a similar post in England. He ended up as a maths teacher at Queenswood College in Hampshire. It is here that Tyndall's character and scientific ambition really began to show themselves.

Having hauled himself up by his bootstraps to a fairly comfortable position, Tyndall realised that Queenswood College wasn't going to satisfy him intellectually. Together with a colleague, Edward Frankland, Tyndall travelled to Germany and enrolled himself at the great age of twenty-eight in the University of Marburg, where his tutor was Herr Bunsen, after whom the laboratory burner is named.

Although his first scientific paper was on the 'Phenomena of a Water Jet', Tyndall settled into some pretty obscure physics. He was particularly interested in the effects of pressure on crystals, which sounds rather dull but led him to work in Wales on how slate cleaves, and then to the Alps where the way glaciers move and crack puzzled physicists:

The John Tyndall restaurant in Carlow.

how can apparently solid ice flow like a river? Perhaps the most dramatic outcome of this work was Tyndall's transformation into an accomplished Alpinist. He loved the mountains, and became one of the first men to scale the Matterhorn, and was the first to climb the Weisshorn in Switzerland. Yet none of this merited any public acclaim. All that was to change thanks to a brilliant lecture he gave in 1853.

Tyndall was invited to deliver one of the prestigious Friday lectures at the Royal Institution in London, where the great Michael Faraday was in charge. The lecture, whose title 'On the Influence of Material Aggregation upon the Manifestations of Force' is meaningless to most of us, was delivered on 11 February. It produced an extraordinary impression, and in May of the same year he was unanimously chosen as Professor of Natural Philosophy in the Royal Institution, working alongside Faraday.

This dramatic transformation seems to have resulted from Tyndall's brilliant performance in public. He was a great experimental scientist – but an outstanding demonstrator. He devised working experimental demonstrations of scientific ideas and techniques that immediately impressed and thrilled both scientists and the public. If he'd been alive today, he would no doubt have had his own television series!

Some of his demonstrations have become classics. To show the idea of resonance, he had a piano installed in the basement of the Royal Institution below the main lecture theatre. Upstairs he had a cello on a long pole, which passed through a hole in the floor and connected to the sounding board of the piano. When someone played the piano downstairs, the cello seemed magically to play itself, the strings resonating to the notes played on the piano. The hole in the floor is still there.

Another idea that interested him was 'total internal reflection', an optical phenomenon where light travelling through a piece of glass does not emerge into the air, but is instead reflected back into the glass. To show this, Tyndall invented the light pipe. All you need is a torch and a bucket with two holes. Seal one hole with a clear window, and fill the bucket with water, which will pour out of the remaining hole. Now shine your torch through the window and into the stream of water emerging on the opposite side of the bucket. It is well known that light travels in straight lines – yet it disappears! Instead, if you put your hand into the water, it is lit up by the light trapped in the stream by total internal reflection. Tyndall predicted that this phenomenon could be useful in telecommunication, and indeed that is exactly how fibre-optic cables use light to carry information round corners.

In 1867, when Faraday died, Tyndall took over as the Superintendent of the Royal Institution. Much of his work was to do with the way gases absorb radiation – it was Tyndall who showed that ozone absorbs ultraviolet light. As part of his investigation, he shone beams of light through filtered, very clean air. And he saw nothing. Normally you can see the beam, but no one had really stopped to wonder why. He now knew that the light beam you see from a spotlight or slide projector is in fact light scattered from tiny particles normally present in the air. And then came the bolt from the blue (almost literally). Since sunlight has to pass through air laden with these tiny particles, then surely a great deal of it must be scattered? So why can't we see the beam? Then he realised that we *can* see the light scattered from the sun. Different sized particles tend to scatter light from different parts of the spectrum – larger particles scatter more red, small ones more blue. If the dust in the atmosphere was mainly small, then it would scatter blue light *and that is why the sky is blue!*

Tyndall made his own blue sky to demonstrate this, of course, and you can do the same. By shining a beam of light from a slide projector through a tank of water, you can scatter more and more light by adding a little powdered milk. The tank takes on a distinctly blue appearance from the side, but when you look directly at the projector through the water and particles, it looks first yellow, then orange, then red, as you add milk powder. As the blue light is scattered from the sunlight, what is left looks yellow, which is why the sun is yellow. Adding more milk produces a lovely red glow, just as at sunset you look at the sun through more atmosphere, with more particles in the way.

John Tyndall died after accidentally taking an overdose of chloral hydrate, but left a legacy of great science, and the idea that scientists have a responsibility to make their work interesting to the public.

Tyndall was a brilliant lecturer, and the Irish branch of the Institute of Physics organises a set of Tyndall lectures in schools every year.

FOOD AND DRINK

Every cook knows that innovation happens every day in the kitchen; we all experiment with many of the meals we make. As a result, people are not usually credited with gastronomic inventions – with a few exceptions such as the Bath Oliver biscuit and the sandwich, named after the 4th Earl of Sandwich (1718–92), who did not actually invent lunch, but refused to leave the gambling table for twenty-four hours, and insisted that someone should bring him a piece of beef between two slices of bread. However, in the course of our research for *Local Heroes*, we occasionally come across some surprising tales of heroes entangled in food and drink.

15. FRANCIS BACON, WHO DIED INVENTING THE FROZEN CHICKEN

Francis Bacon was the sixth child of Sir Nicholas Bacon, Keeper of the Great Seal at the court of Elizabeth I. He was born into a position of great privilege, but no money – he was too far down the line to inherit anything. So he turned to the law, and was a professional lawyer all his life. He lived in St Albans, once the Roman town of Verulamium, and celebrated both those names because he became Viscount St Albans and Baron Verulam. He reached the highest office in the land, but seriously fell out with two monarchs; in his spare time, he laid the foundations for modern science – and died inventing the frozen chicken.

Despite his family connections, he had difficulty getting into court. He insisted on offering advice to Queen Elizabeth, and supported laws she didn't like, so it's not surprising he was less than popular. He found himself in the tricky position of having to support the execution for treason of a good friend of his, the Earl of Essex. When James I took over things looked up, and Bacon's brilliant legal mind was rewarded with a succession of posts, culminating in his becoming Keeper of the Great Seal, as his father had been, and Lord Chancellor of England, the most powerful minister in the land. In 1621 he was created Viscount St Albans. But just five days later it all went horribly wrong when he was charged with bribery. The House of Lords fined him £40,000 and banished him from the 'verge of court' – which meant he had to stay 12 miles away from the King at all times, which is a tricky navigational problem. Although the King later did away with the fine and the sentence, this was the end of Bacon's public life and he retired to Gorhambury, his fine Tudor house, to concentrate on his writing.

What really interested him was truth, and in particular scientific truth. He was worried that a lot of supposedly scientific ideas were simply made up. In particular, he was disturbed to find that Tudor science was based largely on the ideas of Aristotle, who had died in 322 BC. Aristotle, tutor to Alexander the Great, had tried to show how knowledge could be obtained. Many of his conclusions – the earth at the centre of the universe, species of animals never changing – have been overturned. But what Bacon objected to was his method – the idea that scientific truth could be found by authority and argument. If you had clever enough men and they discussed something for long enough, the truth would result. Bacon went out of favour in the late nineteenth century because people said he hadn't fully developed the scientific method, but he it was who suggested that evidence, rather than imagination, should be the basis for scientific truth.

Bacon parodied these 'authorities' as spiders – spinning webs from their own substance. What you needed, he said, was evidence from the real world. He set out ways in which you could accumulate evidence, and one of these was by experiment. Suppose you wanted to investigate gravity, and whether something falls because it is pulled by the earth, or has its own tendency to move downward – which was the old Aristotelian idea. He suggested using two clocks, one regulated by springs, the other by weights. Take them to the top of the highest church, and down the deepest mine. If gravity is a property of the weight itself, the clocks won't be

Old Gorhambury House, built by Francis Bacon's father Sir Nicholas Bacon. Queen Elizabeth was not impressed. 'What a little house you have gotten,' she is supposed to have said. Bacon replied that if the house seemed small it was her fault, because she had made him too great.

affected, but if it comes somehow from the earth, then the weight-driven clock will speed up or slow down as you go closer to or further from the centre of the earth. This is a neat example of the 'Scientific Method', where you test a theory by a controlled experiment. In this case the 'control' is the spring-driven clock, which should always run at the same speed.

He summed up his idea neatly: 'Whether or no anything can be known, can be settled not by arguing, but by trying.' In his spare time he began publishing his new ideas. The frontispiece of his book *Novum Organum* shows the Pillars of Hercules, symbolising in the ancient world the limit of man's knowledge, and a ship sailing through into the modern world of knowledge Bacon dreamed of. The Latin inscription means: 'Many shall sail through and knowledge shall be increased.'

Francis Bacon recorded a curious phenomenon; he said that hot water freezes more quickly than cold water. He did not claim this was his discovery; indeed he said it had been known for a long time. However, it's a claim that you can easily test with your own experiments; fill one glass or ice-cube tray with water from the cold tap and an identical one with water from the hot tap, put both in the freezer, and see which is frozen solid first. Why hot water might freeze first is a bit of a mystery. One possibility is that if your freezer is frosted up, the warm glass melts through the frost and gets better contact; another is that a thin 'lid' of ice forms quickly on the cold water, which actually helps to keep some of the heat in by stopping convection currents in the water. But does it depend on the container? It's certainly a fascinating phenomenon, and an example of something you probably wouldn't have discovered simply by argument. Bacon suggested that as well as doing experiments, scientists should rigorously collect and organise data from the natural world, to make sure their ideas match what really goes on.

There are quite a few odd theories surrounding Bacon. Some people think he is the author of Shakespeare's plays – because a mere actor like William Shakespeare couldn't possibly have done it. Others believe that he was in fact a son of Queen Elizabeth herself. I doubt if either theory would stand up to scientific investigation by Bacon himself.

One snowy day in early April 1626, Bacon was travelling through Highgate, then outside London, when he was seized by a sudden scientific impulse. At the foot of Highgate Hill he obtained a chicken from a peasant. He had a life-long interest in heat and cold, and wanted to find out whether cold could be used to preserve meat. So he stuffed the chicken with snow, which was conveniently lying about on the ground. But while he was doing this, he was suddenly taken ill. He was taken to his friend Lord Arundel's place, which was just round the corner. In the carriage he suffered a fit of 'casting' or vomiting, and had to go to bed as soon as he reached the house. And having invented the frozen chicken, he died a few days later on 9 April.

Gorhambury House was demolished in the eighteenth century to make a picturesque ruin for the new mansion that was being built, but the remains are still visible on the Gorhambury Estate in St Albans. Bacon died in the Old Hall on the corner of The Grove and Bacon Lane, at the top of Highgate Hill.

Gorhambury today.

16. NICHOLAS DE CHEMANT'S COMBINED STOVE AND DINING TABLE

London's Soho district is packed with good restaurants and was probably a good place to eat 200 years ago, but Nicholas Dubois de Chemant seems to have been bothered less by the food and more by his cold feet. He was a surgeon dentist, and he lived in Frith Street.

Eating dinner even in posh homes must have been a chilly affair in the 1790s; central heating had not been invented, and a fireplace on one wall wouldn't be much use unless you happened to be sitting right next to it. As an expatriate Frenchman de Chemant wanted to have warm, cosy dinner parties. So he invented a combined stove and dinner table, and because he took out a patent on it, we know his plans in detail. The table could, he said, be round or oval or square, but the crucial features were a hollow centre and a passage through the side. In the middle he put a stove – he said that any stove of about the right size would do. The smoke from the stove went round a long curly flue pipe before it reached the main chimney. And this long curly pipe ran between the legs of the table, so that all the diners could rest their feet on it.

Result: warm feet, cosy chat, intimate social intercourse – just the thing for the eighteenth-century dinner party. Meanwhile the passage through the side of the table allowed one of the servants to get in and stoke up the fire in the stove, if anyone felt even the faintest chilliness of the feet!

These days the Frith Street restaurants are heated, and de Chemant's stove is no longer needed.

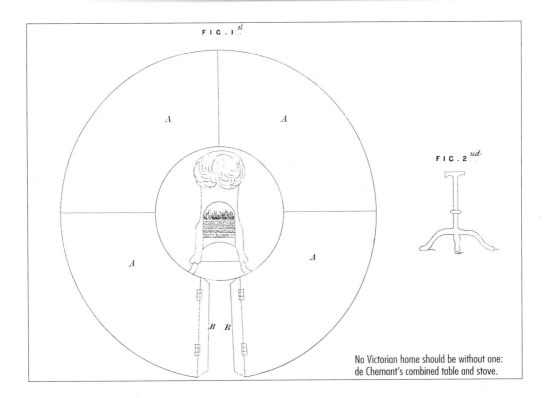

FIG.1st

FIG.2nd

No Victorian home should be without one: de Chemant's combined table and stove.

17. JOSEPH BRAMAH'S BEER ENGINE

Silkstone in South Yorkshire is famous for two things; first, coal, which they've been digging out of the ground for a thousand years, and second, an appalling pit disaster. In the churchyard there's a monument to those who died in the Huskar Pit on 4 July 1838. The shocking thing is that the twenty-six dead were all children who worked in the mine. But the other thing that strikes you is the chilling warning on the monument: not to make mines safer, not suggesting that children shouldn't work in dangerous jobs, but pointing out that since you might be called to meet your maker at any time, you had better be in a fit state.

What Silkstone should be famous for is Joseph Bramah – the man who invented a brilliant water-closet, the first unpickable

lock, the whole science of hydraulics and – some might say most important of all – the beer engine. He was born at Stainborough Lane Farm on 2 April 1749, and his father probably expected him to work on the farm, but he became friendly with the local blacksmith and carpenter. Furthermore the story goes that at the age of sixteen he injured his leg 'while jumping at the Annual Feast at Bolton-on-Dearne', and this injury may have prevented him from becoming a farmer. In any case, he became apprenticed to a carpenter. Then, after the disastrous harvest of 1772, he decided to leave Yorkshire to seek his fortune as a cabinet-maker in London.

The aristocracy in the big city were looking for ways to improve their grand homes, and do better than the neighbours, and one of the smart things to have was a water-closet. There was little piped water,

Royal flush: some Bramah toilets are apparently still used by the royal family at Sandringham.

and no real sewers. Most people could not afford to install such things, so the demand for water-closets was limited. Nevertheless owing one showed real class.

In 1775 Alexander Cumming took out the first English patent for a water-closet. Bramah may have come across one of Cumming's closets, for in 1778 he patented his own water-closet, which was a considerable improvement. Cumming's closet had a sliding valve across the bottom of the pan. The user arrived to find a few inches of water in the pan, on top of the valve. Having finished, the user pulled a lever to one side to slide the valve open and release the contents of the pan into the trap below and thence into the sewer. However, the valve tended to get encrusted, making it hard to slide, and since most closets were in outhouse privies, the valve often froze solid in winter, which must have been disastrous.

The Bramah water-closet had a hinged valve in place of the sliding one – so it could not freeze up – and incorporated several other refinements. Pulling the handle to open the valve also turned on the water to flush the pan. Pushing it down again closed the valve and activated a neat delay mechanism in the shape of a brass air-cylinder, which kept the water running for about fifteen seconds, so as to fill the pan ready for the next person. Bramah water-closets were rather complex and therefore liable to go wrong, but they were splendidly built in mahogany and brass. Within twenty years he sold 6,000, and they were the best water-closets in the country for about seventy-five years.

As a cabinet-maker, it was natural for Bramah to be concerned with locks. Security was clearly a problem and the Society of Arts offered a prize for the best lock. Unfortunately most of the 'unpickable' locks entered were nothing of the kind, and according to the records Bramah himself picked one in just fifteen minutes. Most locks of the time were 'warded' locks, in which an obstacle called a 'ward' prevented the key from turning. The right key had a complex-shaped cut-out which fitted over the ward, and so was able to open the lock.

The trouble was that the tricky part of the lock was accessible from the outside, and anyone could take a wax impression of such a lock and make a new key. Bramah realised that a secure lock would have nothing in the key-hole to reveal what key would open it. He came up with a most elegant secure lock whose exterior revealed nothing about the cryptic parts within. Bramah locks became highly fashionable, and people used to wear the tiny keys round their necks as status symbols. Demand soon outstripped supply, and he had to introduce mass-production for the first time in precision engineering. Before then every lock had been an individual item, with no part from one being of any use in another.

In order to make his locks in large numbers he hired a young man called Henry Maudslay, who designed and built the machines to manufacture the locks, ran Bramah's Denmark Street workshop, married Bramah's housekeeper, Sarah Tindale, and had four children. But even after eight years of service Maudslay was still paid only 30 shillings a week, and he quite reasonably asked his boss for a rise. Bramah (a Yorkshireman) said no, so Maudslay left, set up his own business in Wells Street, and went on to become the father of precision engineering.

In 1790 Joseph Bramah issued a challenge. On a lock in the window of his workshop there was engraved:

The artist who can make an instrument that will pick or open this lock shall receive 200 guineas the moment it is produced. Applications in writing only please.

At that time, 200 guineas was an enormous amount of money: a vast reward for the simple task of picking a lock. And sure enough, the Bramah lock was eventually picked by an American called Hobbs. However, it took him forty-four hours spread over sixteen days – and he did not manage it until 1851, more than sixty years after the challenge, and thirty years after Joseph Bramah's death! The Bramah locks were so good that the expression 'a real Bramah' entered the English language, meaning anything ingenious and beautifully made.

For some people, however, Bramah's most important contribution to society was the beer engine. When he went into a pub and ordered a pint of beer, the landlord had to send a boy down to the cellar to fetch it in a jug. Frequently the boy felt he had to check the beer, and would emerge twenty minutes later slightly wobbly, with only half a jug of beer, having drunk the landlord's profits. Joseph Bramah was determined to put this right. So in 1797 he patented 'Certain methods of Retaining, Clarifying, Preserving and Drawing off all kinds of Liquors commonly used for the beverage of mankind, more especially those Liquors called Malt Liquors, such as Porter, Ale, Beer etc., together with sundry improved casks and implements necessary to give the contrivance full effect'.

Joseph Bramah's beer engine was a barrel with straight sides, into which fitted a piston with a leather seal to keep it beer-tight. The piston had a great weight on top, which put the beer under pressure, and pushed it up a pipe which led from the bottom of the barrel to the bar, where beer could be delivered just by opening a tap. What was more, the landlord could keep the cellar door locked, saving his profits and avoiding the evil of what Bramah called 'private drunkenness'. With this device Bramah had invented far more than a rather complicated way to get a pint. He went on to develop the hydraulic press, and these were the first practical uses of a whole new science – we call it hydraulics.

There is an original Bramah water-closet in the Gladstone Pottery Museum near Stoke-on-Trent; you can admire the works in all their brass glory, although you cannot actually use the lavatory! The Bramah lock was so successful that it is still in production, or at least the Bramah Group now offer comprehensive security systems from 30 Oldbury Place, London W1.

18. BEER CLEARED WITH FISH BY WILLIAM MURDOCK

Most of the pioneers featured in this book are unsung heroes. But 'unsung' doesn't really do justice to what happened to the reputation of this man. He was a mechanical genius who had a hand in the invention of the stationary steam engine, the steam locomotive, gas lighting and many other processes, including the clearing of beer. But his place in history has been completely overshadowed by that of his employers.

William Murdock (1754–1839) was from Ayrshire, and may have changed his name from Murdoch to Murdock because the Sassenachs couldn't handle the Scottish form, or it may simply have been that his handwriting wasn't that good and the 'h' looked like a 'k'. Indeed he spent most of his working life in England, and a good deal of it in Cornwall, looking after the engines made by his employers Boulton and Watt, the greatest engineering firm of the eighteenth and early nineteenth centuries. Matthew Boulton, a brilliant businessman, and James Watt, the dour Scots improver of the steam engine, set up at the Soho Foundry in Birmingham. The business was based on Watt's 1769 patent to improve the steam engine (see page 100).

Murdock walked from Ayrshire to Birmingham in 1777 to get a job with Boulton and Watt. He obviously knew about engines, probably from helping his dad, who was a millwright. There is a story that he dropped his hat during the interview with Boulton, and the great man was surprised by the clonk it made on the floor. It turned out to be made of wood, turned on a special lathe Murdock had invented. Whether or not this is true,

Murdock got the job. He must have been first-rate, because he was soon being sent all over the place to erect and maintain the Boulton and Watt engines. Clearly his employers reckoned the firm's reputation was safe with Murdock. The Cornish mines were some of their biggest customers, and so he rented a house in Redruth.

Seven years after starting with Boulton and Watt, Murdock made a machine which ought to have pride of place in the catalogue of great British inventions – the 1784 steam carriage. As a boy in Scotland he had made some sort of mechanical tricycle, decades before the bicycle was invented. But his steam carriage appeared at least twenty years before the first working locomotive, and was definitely a stunning invention. Yet Boulton and Watt did everything in their power to discourage Murdock from developing it. Perhaps they were afraid of losing their best engineer, perhaps it was because Watt was famously sceptical (or jealous) of ideas that were not his own. On one occasion Boulton managed to intercept Murdock on his way to London to patent the steam carriage, and persuaded him that his place was with the Boulton and Watt engines in Cornwall. Whatever the reason, when he realised that his employers weren't going to take up the idea, Murdock let it go. So this brilliant example of Murdock's genius became no more than a mechanical curiosity.

Murdock is probably most famous as a lighting pioneer, being the first man to make gas-lighting a practical proposition. The house in Redruth may have been the first ever lit by gas, but we can't be certain. Less well known is his fishy method for clearing beer. As well as all the stuff that makes beer taste nice – hops and malt and

The carriage that could have brought us steam transport fifteen years earlier — if Matthew Boulton had not persuaded William Murdock to stick to the day job.

so on – the crucial ingredient is yeast, because that makes the alcohol. If you've ever made (or been forced to drink) home-brewed beer, you'll know that in the hands of an expert it can be all right, but sometimes the result is murky and horrible. The cloudiness in beer is mainly caused by the yeast cells, which are small enough to stay suspended in the liquid. In fact, they will generally settle out as a sludge at the bottom – but it takes time, which is fine for home-brew. But commercial brewers need to make their beer drinkable as quickly as possible, and for assistance they turn to the sturgeon. Now you probably know sturgeon as the fish which produces caviar. But even in Murdock's day it had a crucial role in beer-making. Someone had found out that dried Sturgeon swim-bladder will clear beer. Don't ask me how this was discovered – it's difficult to imagine anyone accidentally dropping a dried

sturgeon swim-bladder into a vat of beer – but it's true. The preparation used is called isinglass, and apparently the best sturgeon for this purpose come from Saigon.

It works like this: particles stay suspended in water better if they have an electric charge – positive or negative. Yeast is generally negatively charged. Isinglass is positively charged, so when the two meet the charges cancel and the muck sinks to the bottom. But there is a serious drawback: since each sturgeon has only one swim-bladder, isinglass is incredibly expensive. Murdock got involved with trying to find a cheaper alternative, and the substance he hit upon was not dried swim-bladder, but dried fish skin. Apparently he used to dry them by hanging them on the curtains of his room, much to the understandable displeasure of his landlady.

The customs and excise people weren't very pleased about the fish-skins, accusing brewers who used Murdock's product of

19. JOSEPH BANKS'S CHOWDER

Murdock's cottage, Redruth. He was a tricky tenant, insisting on drying fish skins on the curtains for his beer-clearing experiments.

Sir Joseph Banks was a fat, arrogant, amusing and talented botanist who, as president of the Royal Society, ruled British science for more than forty years. He brought back exotic specimens from all around the world, but the strangest – and most useful – was a recipe from Newfoundland for fish chowder.

Joseph Banks had a house in London and a large estate at Revesby near Lincoln, which he inherited, along with a substantial fortune, when his father died in 1761. His interest in botany started when he was still at school, and continued at Oxford, and he was elected a Fellow of the Royal Society in 1766. He then delighted his mother by announcing that he was going to travel. She assumed he was thinking of the Grand Tour around the cultural capitals of Europe, and was horrified when he explained that was not quite what he had in mind; instead he planned to go to Newfoundland on a fisheries protection vessel, in order to look for plants.

He was horribly seasick, and didn't enjoy the trip much, but he brought home a number of specimens, and a rather jolly account in his journal of some mysterious stuff called chowder that the natives used to eat.

adulterating their beer. There was a court case in which the prosecution tried to belittle Murdock, and showed how disgusting his preparation was, by producing a bottle which had clearly gone off, and stank. Luckily Humphry Davy, the celebrated chemist, who was also a Cornishman, came to his rescue, testifying that there was nothing fishy about Murdock's isinglass, which was perfectly good at clearing beer. The judge found in Murdock's favour, ruling that his invention should be called 'Isinglass made from British fish'.

So next time you drink a pint of beautifully clear beer, why not raise your glass in a toast to the man who, if he had been less modest and deferential, and better treated by his employers, would be recognised as one of the greatest engineers of the industrial revolution.

It is a soup made with a small quantity of salt Pork cut into Small Slices a good deal of fish and Biscuit Boyled for about an hour unlikely as this mixture appears to be Palatable I have scarce met with any Body in this Country Who is not fond of it.

Murdock's cottage in Redruth is occasionally open to the public.

Unfortunately, not being used to doing his own cooking, he failed to write down a proper recipe, but we tried a genuine experiment, starting with a piece of gammon (in place of the salt pork), boiling that in a saucepan half full of water, and then adding in succession pieces of halibut, cod and prawns, all from Newfoundland, which seemed appropriate. We seasoned the mixture and let it simmer for five minutes, and then crumbled into it a packet of dry biscuits. The whole concoction thickened to the consistency of wallpaper paste, and looked rather grey and unappetising, but it tasted wonderful. Do try it yourself!

The trip of Banks's life came in 1768, when he persuaded the First Lord of the Admiralty that he was the right man to go as botanist with Captain James Cook on his scientific voyage around the world. He insisted on taking along another botanist, Dr Solander, two draughtsmen, two servants, and two greyhounds – but he did pay for all their expenses. For this important voyage Cook had been offered a ship of the line, but he chose instead the *Endeavour*, a second-hand coal barge from Whitby, and Banks's quarters were therefore fairly cramped.

The primary objective of the trip was to observe the Transit of Venus from Tahiti on 3 June 1769. They did this successfully, but on the way they had a host of amazing experiences, which Banks described in his extensive journals. They almost died from cold on what was supposed to be a simple exploratory trip in South America. In Tahiti the natives were extremely

Sir Joseph Banks ruled British science for forty years.

friendly, especially the women, and Banks enjoyed himself enormously. However, he was embarrassed when a lovely lady suggested the floor would be comfortable to lie on – but the house had no walls. . . .

One lady invited him to spend the night with her in a canoe. When he woke up he found that all his clothes had been stolen – as had the pair of pistols he had placed in his pockets to protect himself against thieves. He did not say whether he walked back to the *Endeavour* 'wearing' the canoe.

After Tahiti they sailed round much of Australia, collecting and surveying, and then returned to England. Later Banks went to Iceland, but he then settled to a life of luxury at home, becoming a grand patron of science, rather than an active practitioner. He was invited to go round the world with Cook again in 1772, but this time insisted on taking a retinue of fourteen assistants and servants, not to mention two horn-players. In order to accommodate them, a new cabin and a new deck were built on the ship, the *Resolution*, but when she put to sea this extra superstructure made her completely uncontrollable. Cook ordered it all to be removed, and Banks huffily refused to go.

Banks insisted on taking two greyhounds round the world on Cook's *Endeavour*, in 1768. But Cook drew the line at horn players.

Whenever you see a plant labelled xxx Banksii you know it is descended from one of the plants he brought back from his foreign trips. Many of them grow in the Sir Joseph Banks conservatory in Lincoln. And curiously his names were given to an American who went on to set up the world's first department of parapsychology at Duke University, North Carolina, and coined the phrase extra-sensory perception – Joseph Banks Rhine.

20. WILLIAM BANTING'S DIET

William Banting, born in 1797, was a short, fat undertaker and furnisher of funerals in St James's Street, London. As he grew older he became more corpulent; he was only 5 feet 5 inches tall, but by the time he was sixty-five he weighed 14 stone 6 pounds (92 kg), and could no longer tie his own shoelaces. He had to go downstairs backwards, and slowly, to avoid excessive strain on the ankle joints, and with every exertion he 'puffed and blowed' in a most unseemly way. This was most distressing for him, since his job as a smart undertaker required the utmost in decorous behaviour and respectful quietness.

He consulted several doctors, and asked how he could reduce his size. They told him to take plenty of exercise, so he walked long distances, and then tried rowing. He actually rowed a boat for two hours before breakfast every day. But the result was that he grew hungrier and hungrier – and heavier and heavier.

He visited fifty Turkish baths in a vain attempt to sweat off his pounds, and he drank gallons of patent slimming medicines. He visited spas to take the waters. He even – as a desperate resort – tried the new-fangled practice of sea-bathing. None of these things did any good at all. Then, because he was going deaf, he went to Soho Square and consulted Mr William Harvey. Mr Harvey said his deafness was caused by corpulence, and that the remedy was to go on a diet. He told Banting not to eat bread, butter, milk, sugar, beer, soup, potatoes or beans, but to eat mainly lean meat, fish and dry toast.

Banting's Diet

Breakfast	4–6 oz beef, mutton, kidneys, broiled fish, bacon, or any cold meat except pork 1–2 oz dry toast	1 large cup black tea
Dinner	10–12 oz of any fish except salmon, any meat except pork any vegetable except potato 2 oz dry toast fruit out of a pudding any kind of poultry or game	2 or 3 glasses of good claret, sherry, or Madeira but NO champagne, port, or beer
Tea	4–6 oz fruit a rusk or two	1 large cup black tea
Supper	6–8 oz meat or fish, as dinner	1 or 2 glasses claret
Nightcap		1 tumbler gin, whisky, or brandy

This is basically a high-protein, low-carbohydrate diet, although it seems to have been pretty generous with alcohol. Indeed the quantities of everything seem substantial, with three square meals a day, topped off by a nightcap of a tumbler of gin, whisky or brandy – although without any added sugar! In spite of the enormous intake of alcohol, the diet was successful. Within a year, Mr Banting lost more than 3 stone, and he felt better than he had for twenty years. He was so delighted at having lost so much weight by such simple means that in 1863 he wrote a pamphlet called 'A Letter on Corpulence, addressed to the Public'.

This, too, was an immense success. Tens of thousands of copies were bought by others who wished to be slimmer. The word 'Banting' became synonymous with dieting; and 'to bant' became a household phrase – 'I say, you do look well! Are you banting, my dear?' As a result of this, William Banting became quite rich and enormously famous, and thousands of people followed his advice – which seems rather unfair, really, since the advice came in the first place from Mr William Harvey of Soho Square.

So many copies of his pamphlet were sold that many must still exist, but they are hard to find.

21. MARGARET MCMILLAN AND THE INVENTION OF SCHOOL DINNERS

Green Lane First School in Bradford deserves recognition as an important historic site, because it was there that the first real school dinners were cooked and served in 1907.

Margaret McMillan was born in New York of Scottish parents on 20 July 1860, and later moved to England and into politics; in 1889 she began voluntary work for the Labour Party; in 1893 she went to Bradford to campaign for the Labour Party. The first thing she saw was the terrible state of the children; they looked puny, underfed and ill. Lord Shaftesbury had said the children of Bradford were so deformed they looked like the letters of the alphabet, although he didn't say which

Margaret McMillan, moved by the plight of the poor children of Bradford.

letters! Margaret McMillan spotted that this was good political territory and started her 'fight for the slum child'.

Her first campaign was to get the children clean, since many didn't change their clothes for seven or eight months. After much arguing she got the first school baths opened in Wapping Street School in 1897.

Poor people in Bradford usually sent their children to school in the morning without giving them any breakfast, and since there was no dinner at school the kids got hungrier and hungrier all day. Margaret was sure that lack of food and poor health were connected, and she persuaded Parliament to pass the Education (Provision of Meals) Act in 1906. As a result, the country's first school canteen opened in Green Lane on 28 October 1907, and was soon making nutritious meals not only for the Green Lane children but also for children in other schools all over Bradford.

For their school dinners today the Green Lane children get mainly Asian food – curries, samosas, and so on – because many of them are Asian. Ninety years ago they had not just dinner, but three meals a day. For breakfast they were given oatmeal porridge, probably with treacle, and bread and dripping. In the middle of the day they had stew and a sticky pudding, and then at teatime there was a slice of bread and margarine, and a cup of tea.

Margaret McMillan, once called 'Labour Prophetess of the North', died on 29 March 1931. She was a splendid campaigner and pioneer; she started the first nursery schools in Bradford, the first school medical inspections, and the first school baths, but best of all she started school dinners. In particular I remember her for the bread and dripping – I used to love it when I was at primary school.

Green Lane First School is flourishing, and the food there is delicious. Few people in the country can have escaped the gastronomic delights of school dinners!

22. JOE SHERIDAN AND IRISH COFFEE

Shannon airport in the west of Ireland is a surprisingly pioneering place. It is where transatlantic flying really began, where duty-free shopping was invented, and where Joe Sheridan made that crucial aviation innovation – Irish coffee.

Sheridan was born in County Tyrone in 1909. In about 1942 he got a job as a chef at the seaport of Foynes, on the Shannon estuary, a few miles from the present site of Shannon airport. At that time, transatlantic passenger flights were all by flying boat, the idea being that you could land in the water if the weather or fuel consumption got the better of you. Flights left from Botwood, Newfoundland, on the far side, to Foynes, from where passengers got a land transfer or conventional flight to their final destinations.

Being a pioneering transatlantic passenger may have been exciting, but it wasn't as glamorous as everyone hoped. The planes carried twenty-five to thirty people in an unpressurised cabin, on a flight lasting up to eighteen hours. Sometimes planes had to turn back because of bad weather after perhaps four hours of flight. Whether they had made it or not, the passengers would certainly be cold and uncomfortable. Joe Sheridan was working as a chef at Foynes when the catering manager Brendan O'Regan spotted a gap in the market. Surely they could think of a novel way of warming up and improving the mood of the frozen transatlantic passengers while they waited for their onward flights. Could Joe invent something hot, alcoholic and with an Irish flavour?

Thanks to flying boats like this Imperial Airways Shorts S.23 'Caribou', Foynes justifiably called itself 'The centre of the aviation world'.

Joe Sheridan came up with a brand new drink, known as Irish coffee. It consisted of coffee mixed with whiskey, and topped off with half an inch of cream. The idea was to drink the hot coffee through the cold cream – and it is absolutely delicious. But it wasn't quite as simple as it seemed.

After the war conventional planes took over from the flying boats, but they still used Shannon airport to refuel, and Irish coffee continued to be a great hit. In the 1950s a travel writer called Stanford Delaplane from the *San Francisco Chronicle* came through, and liked the Irish coffee so much that he decided to import it to America. He described it to bartender Jack Koeppler at the Buena Vista bar in San Francisco. Here they attempted to recreate the magnificent drink – but without success. He utterly failed to make the cream float, so he had to return to Shannon for a scientific lesson from the master.

There is a bit of a paradox here. In Irish coffee the cream clearly floats on the coffee. But anyone who drinks conventional coffee with cream will know that it is perfectly possible to mix the cream smoothly with the coffee and it doesn't separate out – which is what happened to the unfortunate Mr Delaplane. Joe had a trick and a bit of science to help.

This is how to make proper Irish coffee. Put a measure of whiskey – Irish, of course – into a glass that has been warmed so that it doesn't crack. Then add three lumps or a tablespoon of sugar – they use brown sugar at Shannon airport, but it doesn't really matter. Pour in the coffee to within an inch of the top of the

The author conducting important research at Joe Sheridan's Bar, Shannon airport.

glass. The sugar makes the drink taste yummy – but cunningly also makes the coffee more dense, so the cream floats more easily. The other trick known to Irish coffee drinkers is that you pour on the cream – which should be double, and lightly whipped – over the back of a spoon to discourage mixing, but in the Joe Sheridan Bar at Shannon the cream is thick enough to make this unnecessary.

Joe later went to California, where each year more Irish coffee is consumed in San Francisco alone than in the whole of Ireland. He died in 1962 and is buried within sight of the Golden Gate Bridge.

To reach Shannon airport by road, you have to pass through Limerick, so it seems appropriate to recap the recipe in verse:

Joe Sheridan's cunning hot drink
Is easy to make – if you think
That sugar's propensity
To increase the density
Ensures that the cream doesn't sink!

They serve a wonderful Irish coffee in Joe Sheridan's Bar at Shannon airport.

TRANSPORTS OF DELIGHT

People are generally impatient about getting from A to B; they always want to travel with more speed, more comfort and more style. Until the early 1800s the only real options were by foot, on horseback or in the slow and uncomfortable coaches. However, the advent of steam carriages and steam trains persuaded people that travel was not only necessary but even desirable, and so there appeared a succession of weird and wonderful vehicles. Meanwhile other curious craft were developed for military purposes. Here are the stories of how some of them came about.

23. GEORGE POCOCK'S KITE-POWERED CHARVOLANTS – EVADING THE TOLLS

In 1828 the citizens of Bristol were astonished to see a completely new vehicle sailing along the roads, over the downs and into the hills. 'After many experiments Mr George Pocock', according to the *Annals of Bristol*, 'invented a vehicle somewhat similar in form to the modern tricycle, and found that one of these, capable of carrying four persons, could be drawn by two kites of twelve feet and ten feet in height respectively – the speed attained with a brisk wind being about twenty-five miles an hour.'

George Pocock, brother of artist Nicholas Pocock, opened a school on St Michael's Hill in Bristol, and apparently had some problems with discipline, since he claimed to have invented a patent self-acting ferrule, or spanking machine. However, his kite-powered carriage was a

far more humane device. He called the vehicle a charvolant, and demonstrated one to George IV at Ascot races that year. The charvolant would sail easily downwind and with slight modifications could be made to tack across the wind and even slightly into it. In 1836 the British Association for the Advancement of Science met in Bristol, and Pocock's charvolants were much admired. Among those who enjoyed a ride over the downs was Prince George of Cumberland, later King of Hanover.

Pocock also promoted the uses of kites for other things, including rescues. To demonstrate his ideas he put his young daughter Martha in an armchair and flew her from the beach up to the top of a high cliff. She survived the ordeal, and went on to become the mother of cricketer W.G. Grace.

The *Liverpool Mercury* recorded that Pocock used kites to pull a ferry boat across the Mersey, and said that with the largest kites and a good wind, a boat 'would be able to make the passage from and to Birkenhead, whatever might be the state and strength of the tide', and that the boat could be drawn in any direction 'less than five points from the wind'.

According to *A treatise on the Aeropleustic Art, or Navigation in the Air, by means of Kites or buoyant sails, with a description of the Charvolant, or Kite Carriage*, 'Mile after mile, in succession, has been performed at the rate of twenty miles an hour, timing it by chronometer in hand. A mile has frequently been performed, over a heavy road, in two minutes and three quarters. Let it be noticed, that the wind was not furious, neither were the kites additionally powerful for the bad state of the roads . . .

'That the swiftness of movement should

almost prevent breathing, is certain, if going against the wind; but when travelling at such a rate, it is with the wind, and thus a perfect calm is enjoyed. One evil, however, it was supposed did arise from its velocity – loss of appetite; for on one occasion, when pulling up at a house of call seventeen miles from Bristol, some little concern was felt by the party when not one of them was disposed to take any refreshment. . . . However . . . on looking at the chronometer, they discovered that their travelling pace, up hill and down, had been sixteen miles within the hour: of course there could be little disposition to hunger so soon after a plentiful repast at home.'

The Pocock family travelled by charvolant for many years, and apart from the sheer fun discovered one great advantage over more conventional forms of transport on the turnpikes. The government had introduced heavy tolls on all carriages, partly to encourage people to use the railways which were then spreading across the country – the Great Western Railway reached Bristol in 1841. There

For years Pocock avoided paying tolls in his 'Charvolant' because the law hadn't anticipated kite-powered carriages!

were tolls laid down for steam carriages, for horse-drawn carriages and for ox-carts, but there were no tolls specified for charvolants, and so the Pococks used the turnpikes for free.

The Bristol Kitestore (0117 974 5010) has kite-powered buggies for sale, and sometimes also for hire.

It is not clear what advantage a kite-powered boat would have over one with sails — maybe Pocock did it for fun.

24. KIRKPATRICK MACMILLAN AND THE FIRST PEDAL-POWERED BICYCLE

Courthill Smithy in the parish of Keir, about 14 miles from Dumfries, has more plaques on it than the average blacksmith's premises, and amazingly they all claim that right there Kirkpatrick MacMillan invented the bicycle. It is rather surprising to find that one person invented the bike, and more so that the invention came so late – in 1839, ten years after Stephenson's *Rocket* and thirty-five years after the first steam locomotives. What's more, tricycles were around in 1828 (see page 60). But did MacMillan really do it?

Kirkpatrick MacMillan was born in Keir in September 1812, and became a blacksmith like his dad. He probably went off to work on a neighbouring farm, got a job as a coachman, and at twenty-two became an assistant to the blacksmith of the Duke of Buccleuch. Eventually he returned to Courthill to assist his father and took over the business when his dad retired in 1851.

The story of the bicycle is a bit more complicated. Some people think it went like this: in Germany Karl von Drais had invented the hobby-horse in 1817. It had no pedals, so you sat astride it and pushed with your feet on the ground and scooted along. This was a big craze for a few years, and it is quite possible that MacMillan saw one of these machines. Later, in the 1860s, pedal-driven bicycles were made by Michaux in Paris and were known as bone-shakers or velocipedes,

MacMillan's bike was hard enough to ride down the road, never mind to Glasgow where MacMillan managed to have the first ever traffic accident involving a bicycle.

depending on whether you were more impressed by their comfort or by their speed. The 'ordinary', high bicycle or penny-farthing came along in about 1870. But according to supporters of the Courthill blacksmith, Kirkpatrick MacMillan built the first powered bicycle much earlier, in 1839.

At this time the only bicycle around was the hobby-horse, and MacMillan's brilliant realisation was that it would actually be better to power the machine via some sort of mechanism, rather than using the feet directly on the ground. So MacMillan's machine was wooden like a hobby-horse. It had wooden wheels with solid tyres but with a treadle-powered crank mechanism acting on the rear wheel. This consisted of two iron rods (he was an ironmonger, after all) hinged from just below the handlebar, one on each side. At the bottom of the rods were the pedals, which in turn were connected to the rear wheel cranks by a second pair of iron rods.

Riding it feels pretty peculiar to someone used to a modern bike – it's more like a foot-powered sewing machine. You have to get it rolling, and then push the pedals forwards, away from you, rather than downwards. It feels very heavy and steering is quite difficult because the cranks restrict the movement of the front wheel. Apparently the original machine weighed half a hundredweight, but in spite of this MacMillan frequently rode into Dumfries in less than an hour, which is impressive, to say the least. But it is without question a powered bicycle.

The critics say it is not the precursor of the modern bike. Drive to the back wheels didn't come into serious use for another forty years, and the treadles were a blind alley. However, we are used to pioneers who were ahead of their time. The more serious question concerns the evidence. And there isn't much evidence that MacMillan really built and rode such a machine – except a wonderful article in the *Glasgow Argus* of 1842 which reports that a gentleman of Dumfriesshire had ridden a velocipede 40 miles from Old Cumnock to Glasgow in five hours, and there among a crowd of spectators had mounted the pavement and knocked over a small child. Luckily the child was unhurt and the gentleman was fined only five shillings.

Unfortunately the article does not mention MacMillan by name, nor does it say that the velocipede was a bicycle, and by the social standards of the day he was not a gentleman. And it does say the wheels were turned by *hand*. On the other hand, in the area round Courthill, MacMillan's claim is recognised.

He didn't bother to patent the design and indeed seems to have done little with it, but others saw his bike, copied it and sold the copies for £6 or £7. Apparently Gavin Dalzell of Lesmahagow copied the MacMillan machine in 1846, and his design became so well known that for years *he* was regarded as the inventor of the bicycle! So there is some controversy about who actually invented the bicycle. If it was Kirkpatrick MacMillan, the blacksmith of Courthill, he should surely be saluted as a mechanical genius who in the age of steam was the first to harness human power in a vehicle.

Courthill smithy is now a private house, albeit with plaques on the wall. It stands a few miles south-west of Thornhill. There is a replica of the MacMillan bike in the Bicycle Museum, Drumlanrig Castle.

25. JOHN BOYD DUNLOP AND THE PNEUMATIC TYRE

This is the apparently straightforward story of the vet who transformed cycling comfort by ripping up one of his wife's old dresses, nailing it to a wooden disc and thus inventing the pneumatic tyre. Unfortunately, Dunlop's claim to this great invention turns out to be rather controversial.

John Boyd Dunlop was born on 5 February 1840 in Dreghorn in Scotland. He studied animal medicine, and went to Belfast to set up as a vet in 1869. For twenty years he ran a successful practice in Gloucester Street. He had a son, Johnny, who rode to school on a tricycle and liked to race with his friends. But the streets in Belfast were rough – they were made of cobbles, with tramlines crossing them, and in those days bicycle and tricycle tyres were made of solid rubber. Anyone who has tried solid tyres will confirm that it would have been most uncomfortable. Young Johnny complained that his bottom was sore.

His dad John Boyd wondered if he could

Dunlop did not invent the first pneumatic tyre – but he invented the one that worked.

smooth the ride by putting a cushion of air between the bike and the road, and he decided to build a prototype. Apparently he was for some reason or other used to handling and using rubber, so he got hold of a thin rubber tube and glued the ends together with rubber solution. To inflate the tyre, he incorporated a valve from a football, and so made himself an inner tube. The next challenge was to fix the tyre to the rim of the wheel, and he achieved this, and protected the delicate rubber tube, thanks to one of his wife's old dresses, which he ripped into strips and wrapped over the inner tube, nailing it into his prototype wooden wheel.

Then, rather brilliantly, he conducted a scientific test. He took his prototype wheel, and a similar one with a solid tyre, and rolled them along his cobbled back yard. The solid one soon fell over, but the pneumatic tyre rolled to the end and bounced off the back wall. So he made pneumatic tyres for the back wheels of Johnny's tricycle, and sent him off to school. The first field reports were highly favourable: Johnny could now beat his friends in races – and in comfort!

What was surprising was that the new tyre was not only more comfortable, it actually went faster. The reason the pneumatic tyre works so well is that the air cushion in effect irons out the little bumps in the road. Technically, it reduces the 'unsprung weight' to zero. When the solid wheel goes over a bump, the whole wheel (and thus the whole bike) is thrown into the air, which is uncomfortable for the rider and also uses energy. When the pneumatic tyre goes over the same bump, the tyre squashes a bit but doesn't rise. So you hardly feel a jolt, and although some energy is lost – and goes to heat the air inside the tube – it loses much less energy than is necessary to lift the bike and rider off the ground. The squishiness of the tyre does increase its rolling resistance, because every movement of the tyre on the road deforms the rubber – it's like riding up a very slight hill all the time – but you lose much less energy like this than you do if you have to lift the whole bike and rider on every bump.

John Boyd Dunlop thought there might be money in his tyre, so he demonstrated it to some Belfast businessmen, and then applied for a patent in July 1888. He got tyres made in Edinburgh, with bikes from Edlin and Co. in Belfast, who had made Johnny's tricycle. There were some real technical problems to be overcome, like getting special forks made to fit his chunky tyres. But the biggest problem was the macho attitude of cyclists; many serious cyclists thought only namby-pambies would ride on safety bicycles as opposed to the fast but deadly 'high bicycle' or penny-farthing, let alone on cushioned wheels. So Dunlop went straight to the top. Willie Hume, Captain of the Belfast Cruiser Cycle Club, had had a terrible fall from a penny-farthing so he rode safety bikes. Dunlop persuaded him not only to ride on pneumatic tyres but to enter a race with them. The great race happened on 18 May 1889, on the Queen's College playing fields. Everyone laughed at Willie Hume when he turned up on his inflatable tyres, but they stopped laughing when he won the race. Two of the losers in that race were the Du Cros brothers. They managed to get hold of bikes with pneumatic tyres, took them over to England, and in the summer of 1889 they won every race they were allowed to enter.

Their dad was William Harvey Du Cros, a Dublin paper merchant. He saw the potential for these tyres, and in 1896 he bought the business for three million pounds. After various deals and struggles it became the Dunlop Rubber Company, with the white-bearded portrait of John Boyd Dunlop as its logo. Tyres were at first still fixed to the rim of the wheel – conventionally spoked now, rather than wooden – by wrapping canvas impregnated with rubber solution round the inner tube and rim, permanently fixing the tyre. This skilled job was done by the company, so cycle manufacturers from England who wanted pneumatic tyres had to send men over on the ferry with bare rims to be fitted up. Dunlop himself took no part in the business, moving to Dublin where eventually he had an interest in a drapers. So although he lived comfortably, it was not Dunlop who made the real money from his invention.

This is where you have to be rather careful, because there is a dispute as to whether it is really 'his' invention at all. To the distress of the company, it turned out that Dunlop wasn't the first person to invent the pneumatic tyre; one had actually been patented forty-three years earlier by another Scot called Robert Thompson. So what are the facts? The titles of the patents reveal what the two men were trying to do. Thompson's patent is dated 10 December 1845, and is for 'An improvement in carriage wheels which is also applicable to other rolling bodies'. Dunlop's patent of 31 October 1888 is for 'An improvement in Tyres of wheels for bicycles, tricycles, or other road cars'. Thompson's wheels were big and heavy, intended for carriages. The problem was they were so cumbersome

The Dunlop Company went from bikes to cars and from strength to strength.

that the idea didn't catch on. In Dunlop's day the bicycle as we know it was just becoming available, and he saw this as the important area. Perhaps Thompson was just ahead of his time.

Both men described the use of a rubber tube encased in canvas, though only Dunlop specifies in detail how it is to be attached to the wheel, or how air is to be introduced (through a non-return valve). Thompson merely says that air is passed through a pipe 'fitted with an air-tight screw cap'; he doesn't say how you stop air escaping as you tighten it. In summary, the idea of a pneumatic tyre was clearly patented first by Thompson, although we have Dunlop to thank for the word 'pneumatic'. Dunlop thought of applying it to bicycles and other light vehicles, where Thompson had rather generally applied it

to locomotives, carriages and other road vehicles. Dunlop subsequently modified his patent, to make it clear that he was claiming the *method* for making and using the tyre, not the idea of using air.

So Dunlop's invention looks a little tainted – especially if you believe the claim of some supporters of Thompson that the families actually knew each other in Scotland. But it seems unlikely Dunlop would have applied for a patent knowing that someone else had already taken one out – indeed you might have expected the Patent Office to have picked this up. In the end, it was Dunlop rather than Thompson who brought the world the pneumatic tyre, thanks in part to his sore-bottomed son.

The premises of John Boyd Dunlop's veterinary practice have become a car park, but the pneumatic tyre is everywhere.

26. MIKAEL PEDERSEN AND BIKES TIED TOGETHER WITH STRING

The *Dursley Gazette* for 21 October 1893 reported:

A New Bicycle. Mr M. Pedersen of Dursley, with that ingenuity for which he is known, has recently constructed a safety bicycle of remarkable character. Its weight is only 19 pounds and the maker has tested the strength in an extraordinary way, he having ridden it up Whiteway.

Whiteway is the fearsome hill that rises through the beech woods to the east of Dursley in Gloucestershire. It is one of those hills that if you ride up it on a bicycle you wish you hadn't! In 1896 the Cyclists Touring Club instructed a local wheelwright to put up a sign on Whiteway reading: NOTICE TO CYCLISTS. THIS HILL IS DANGEROUS. Certainly I should not like to come down it without brakes and with my feet on handlebars, which was the style in Pedersen's day.

Mikael Pedersen was born on 25 October 1855 at Marbjeg, near Copenhagen in Denmark, the eldest of seven children. He became an apprentice in a local firm making agricultural equipment, and while he was there invented a self-clearing threshing machine and a new bicycle, the parts for which were made in the factory. He also invented a centrifugal cream separator, which made him money and got him invited to England by Mr Lister of Dursley. He moved over to England in March 1893, and in September the same year patented his new bicycle.

Behind his house he set up a small factory

PEDERSEN TEAM (MR. JORGENSEN LEADING, MR. MELLERUP THIRD FROM LEFT) BEING PACED BY MR. PEDERSEN, THE INVENTOR

The four-man Pedersen. The inherent lightness and strength of his system allowed Pedersen to push back the limits of bicycle design.

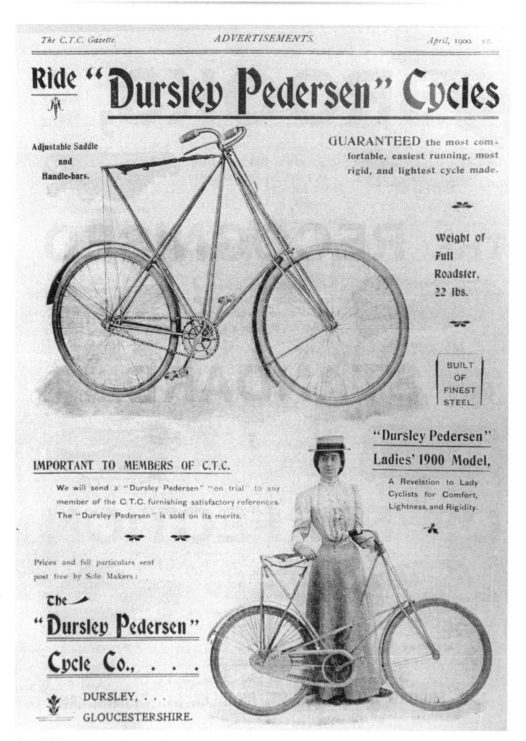

The unlikely but ingenious Pedersen bicycle. You sat on a sling, which tensioned the slender frame.

to make bicycles; the early machines were made of wood, but in 1897 he switched to metal. The startling new concept behind Pedersen cycles was that they were all in tension. The frame was made of many very thin tubes, most of which seemed to meet at a point behind the handlebars, and the ends of the tubes were tied together with fine wires. Even the saddle, instead of being perched on the end of a rigid saddle tube, was slung on a hammock-like strap, which provided the rider with soft suspension.

Soon these new cycles began to make their mark. On 14 November 1898 Harry Goss Green set a new record on a Pedersen from London to Brighton and back in 6 hours, 8 minutes and 11 seconds. In 1900 he broke several more records: London–Liverpool (203 miles) in 11 hours; World 100 miles in 4 hours 41 minutes; London–York (197.5 miles) in 10 hours 19 minutes; and World 12 hours, 225 miles.

Many other remarkable tales arose, such as that of the Revd Sidney Swan, who rode from his parish in Carlisle all the way to London (301 miles) in less than twenty-four hours, even though he was cut and bruised when knocked off by a dog near Towcester. Many thousands of Pedersen cycles were made in Dursley, and some are still being made today, both in England and on the Continent.

In 1896 Mikael was President of the Dursley Star rugby football club and the Dursley Star cricket club. He married three times – to Laura, Dagmar, and Ingeborg. Unfortunately the business eventually failed, and he went back to Denmark, where he died on 22 October 1929. But his bones were brought back to Dursley in 1996.

A blue plaque marks Pedersen's house in Dursley, and Pedersen bicycles are still obtainable, both modern replicas and originals.

27. THE JOSEPH ALOYSIUS HANSOM CAB

You might have thought that a man whose invention becomes so well known that it takes his name would be a pretty good bet in business – think of the Duke of Wellington and his boots. But going into business with Joseph Aloysius Hansom, architect and inventor of the Hansom cab, would almost certainly have been a disaster.

Joseph Hansom was born in York on 26 October 1803, the son of a joiner. Although he worked in his father's business for a while, he showed enough promise as a designer for his articles of apprenticeship to be allowed to lapse, and he took out new ones with a firm of architects. He went to night school to improve his education, and was soon doing pretty well. He married and joined a firm in Halifax, where he first became enthusiastic about the Gothic style which became his trademark. A staunch Catholic, he specialised in churches.

His big break came in 1831, when he won the competition to design Birmingham's Town Hall. This should have been his moment of triumph, but it turned to disaster. As well as designing the town hall, he was contracted to build it, which he did in 1833 – but the terms of his contract meant that he personally had to stand bond for the builders. Something went wrong, and he was declared bankrupt.

Hansom must have been a resilient character, because in the following year he applied to patent the 'Construction of Carriages'. In fact the carriages that

Hansom's original design for a cab had a complicated door built in to the huge wheels to let passengers in and out.

appear in Patent 6733 aren't the ones you see in Sherlock Holmes films, with the driver at the back; those were modified carriages invented later, but the original safety cab was such a novel idea that the name of its inventor became attached to the more successful versions that followed. Hansom states his aim: that 'the wheels be of much larger dimensions, and the body parts of the carriages situated much nearer the ground, than has been hitherto conveniently possible'.

Not only was such a specification not 'conveniently possible', it was quite contradictory: if you make the wheels of a carriage bigger, the body will have to be further from the ground. Hansom got around this problem by dispensing with

the axle and attaching the wheels instead to the sides of the body, which was strengthened for the purpose. He could then specify enormous wheels, which sailed smoothly over the rutted streets of London and other cities, and yet lower the centre of gravity of the carriage by setting the body closer to the ground, making it more stable than a conventional small-wheeled carriage. He also invented a wagon of a similar type, in which the whole body could be detached from the wheels – a forerunner of the container system used by lorries today.

There was a slight problem in Hansom's eyes: getting in and out. A conventional carriage was boarded from the side, but the Hansom's sides were entirely obscured by its huge wheels. In fact, it proved quite possible to arrange for access from the front, but Hansom had a more daring plan. In the patent he suggested that 'in certain cases the wheels be dispensed with altogether'. What he had in mind was not dragging the cabs around, but a new sort of wheel in which the centre remained stationary, and only the rim moved on roller bearings. In the centre of the wheel was a door, so that passengers actually entered the cab through the wheel. Not surprisingly, this more radical Hansom never caught on. But the basic design did, and Hansom sold it for £10,000. Not a penny of this was ever paid, as the firm got into difficulties. Eventually Hansom himself stepped in to sort things out, got the firm back into order and received a fee of £300 – the only money he was ever paid for his invention.

He turned instead to publishing, feeling that the building trade needed a journal. *The Builder* first came out in 1842, but there was not enough capital in the project and Hansom had to withdraw, taking a small fee from the publishers. He returned to architecture, and especially churches. His most famous are St Walburga's Church in Preston, Lancashire, with its 306 foot high spire, and Plymouth Cathedral, though there are many others all over Britain and also in Australia and South America. Hansom died on 29 June 1882, a successful architect of the new Gothic style; but think how much more successful he would have been with a little more luck – or judgement – in business.

Hansom cabs are rare, but look out for his churches – and note the temple-like Birmingham Town Hall.

28. HARRY FERGUSON'S TRACTOR, THE 'WEE FERGIE'

Some people become Local Heroes by a single shattering stroke of brilliance, others by a string of elegant theories. One Ulsterman will be remembered for neither of those reasons, but because for forty years he designed agricultural machinery better than anyone else in the world. His name was Harry Ferguson. He was born on 4 November 1884 in Growel, near Hillsborough, County Down, the fourth son in a family of eleven children. At the age of fourteen he went to work on the family farm. Later he went to Belfast to join his brother repairing cars and bikes. Then he caught the flying bug – Blériot had just flown across the Channel – and became the first man in Ireland to build his own plane, which he managed to fly on 31 December 1909.

In 1913 he started selling cars and tractors from May Street in Belfast, and it was there, in what is now a pub, that in 1917 he designed his first plough. It must have seemed a bit boring and down to earth – literally – after flying about in a plane, but this was where his fame and fortune lay. In 1916 there had been a desperate food shortage, and the Irish Board of Agriculture asked Ferguson to improve tractor ploughing methods, and increase productivity – and that is exactly what he did for the rest of his life!

He and his designer Willie Sands travelled extensively around Ireland demonstrating tractors to reluctant farmers, who thought they would never replace the horse. As a result Ferguson and Sands learned a great deal both about ploughing methods and about what types of tractors and ploughs were available. The tractors were great big monsters with

Harry Ferguson (left) with Henry Ford, who regarded him as a genius.

simple tow-bars at the back. If you wanted to plough, you hitched your heavy plough on to the tow-bar, and pulled it across the field. Basically, the tractor was designed simply to replace the horse and pull things.

There were two major problems with this. First, you had little control over the depth of ploughing. The plough ran on its own wheels, and you had to preset the depth. It all had to be extremely heavy to keep the ploughshares down, and it simply sank in according to its weight and the softness of the ground, so your furrows would be much deeper in the softer bits of the field.

Because the plough was so heavy, the tractor needed tremendous power to pull it along, and the only way to get more power in soft ground was to make the tractor immensely heavy too. Many weighed more than 3 tons. As a result they were unwieldy and inefficient, and used masses of fuel just getting themselves about. Worse, the tractors and ploughs were dangerous. If your plough hit a large rock under the surface, the nose of

the plough would dig in, the back wheels of the tractor would keep turning; the whole thing would jack-knife and the tractor would turn right over backwards. Many tractor drivers were killed in this way.

Harry realised that he could make the system much safer by using a three-point linkage. The main towing force was transmitted by two bottom links, as before, but he introduced a rigid top link. This solved both the previous problems. First, when the plough hit an obstacle it couldn't dig in, and the tractor couldn't tip over backwards, because the top bar prevented any jack-knife. All that happened was that the back wheels spun until they lost grip. Second, the driver could control the depth of the furrow with the top link. Extend it a bit, and it pushed the ploughshares down into the earth; pull it, and it lifted them nearer the surface. It was a really brilliant innovation, and formed the basis of what came to be called the Ferguson System.

Armed with this basic idea, Ferguson set

about redesigning the whole mechanism. Instead of having a tractor and a whole lot of things to tow behind it, he thought of the tractor and plough as a single unit. There was no need to have wheels on the plough; just think of it as an extension of the tractor. He devised a hydraulic link to adjust the plough in mid-furrow, and he made both the tractor and the plough as light as possible – he got them down to about half the weight they had been before.

Harry Ferguson was a stickler for detail. Even in the early days he insisted that everything in the workshop had to be in exactly the right place. If even a single nut and bolt was misplaced then he refused to begin work. Vehicles in the garage had to be lined up precisely on chalk marks, and the whole premises were kept scrupulously clean. Every mechanic had to wear clean overalls, and would be reprimanded for not changing them during the day if they got dirty.

Later, he made all his employees carry pencil and paper at all times, in case they suddenly had a useful idea. The notebook had to be in the left jacket pocket, and the pencil within easy reach of the right hand. Ferguson often stopped people in the corridors and asked to see their notebooks.

In 1936 Harry Ferguson went into partnership with David Brown of Huddersfield, and 1,250 Brown-Ferguson tractors were built. However, Ferguson was stubborn and dogmatic, and Brown found him too difficult to work with, so the partnership broke up.

Ferguson went off to America and showed his tractor and plough to the king of cars, Henry Ford. In 1919 Ford had offered him a job, but Harry refused; Ferguson was not for hire. However, when he went back in 1939 they went into partnership, on an unwritten handshake agreement, and between 1939 and 1947, 300,000 Ford Ferguson tractors were built in Dearborn, Michigan. Every serious farmer had one, even President Franklin Delano Roosevelt. Unfortunately, when Henry Ford died, his grandson Henry Ford II refused to recognise the unwritten agreement, and cut Ferguson out. Ferguson sued him for $340 million. Four years and $3 million later, he accepted an out-of-court settlement of $9.25 million.

In 1946 Ferguson started making his own TE20 tractors in Coventry. This tractor, the 'Wee Fergie', was the most successful of all; in the next ten years, half a million were made. They became the basic piece of equipment on almost every farm in Britain – easy to drive and maintain, small enough to plough the tiniest field.

Ferguson insisted on simplicity in every aspect of his machines. Every bolt and nut and shaft on the Wee Fergies had a diameter of either $^{11}/_{16}$ in or $1^{1}/_{16}$ in. Each tractor was supplied with a spanner $^{11}/_{16}$ at one end and $1^{1}/_{16}$ at the other. The spanner was 10 inches long; this was the standard distance between furrows, so the farmer could use the length of the spanner to check his ploughshares. And the spanner was marked in inches and centimetres, so that among other things he could use it as an accurate dipstick to check the fuel – there was no other fuel gauge.

In 1953 Ferguson went into partnership with the Canadian firm Massey Harris to form the agricultural giant Massey-Ferguson. Massey-Ferguson tractors formed the basis of the Sno-cats that took Sir Edmund Hillary to the South Pole, and the company has been important ever since.

There's a twist in the tail of this tale. In 1948, wanting to promote his new TE20, Ferguson ordered some scale models from Nicholas Kove, who had just started using the first injection-moulding equipment to make plastic combs. Kove had no new materials – this was just after the war – so he made the model tractor bodies from old fountain pens, and the rubber tyres from the insulation taken from waste electrical cables. They came out in whatever colours had been available – red, cream, blue. Furthermore, Kove could not afford to assemble them, so he sent the tractors out in kit form. Nicholas Kove's company was called Airfix, and the Wee Fergie was the very first Airfix model.

The model that tractor salesmen had to make up themselves – it was the first ever Airfix kit.

Harry Ferguson summed up his philosophy in one sentence: 'Beauty in engineering is that which performs perfectly the function for which it was designed, and has no superfluous parts.'

He was a hero because he revolutionised world agriculture by application of simple scientific principles to the art of ploughing.

Wee Fergies are still used on thousands of farms, and perhaps the most fitting memorial to Harry Ferguson comes from Wales: in the Welsh language, the word for 'tractor' is fergie.

29. WILLIAM ASHBEE TRITTON AND HIS TANK 'LITTLE WILLIE'

At the beginning of this century, military experts were convinced that the next war would be won by the cavalry, who galloped so fast they could run rings round anyone on the ground. But the experts reckoned without the invention of the machine-gun. Machine-guns simply mowed down the cavalry.

Infantry were able to escape machine-gun fire by digging themselves deep trenches, but then they were stuck, and in the first two years of trench warfare in the First World War no unit moved more than 3 miles. There was complete stalemate, brought about by machine-guns, trenches, barbed wire and mud. What they needed was a whole new method of warfare.

The Duke of Wellington claimed the battle of Waterloo was won on the playing fields of Eton. Perhaps a tank historian may suggest the First World War was won at the White Hart Hotel in Lincoln, because every week for many months Lieutenant Walter Wilson and William Ashbee Tritton met there to discuss the tank.

William Ashbee Tritton was born in Islington on 19 June 1875, the son of William Birch Tritton and his wife Ellen Ashbee. He became an engineer, and after working for various companies moved as general manager to Fosters in Lincoln, who made agricultural machinery. In 1911 he became Managing Director.

The First Lord of the Admiralty was a young chap called Winston Churchill – this was twenty-five years before he

Tritton's tank broke the deadlock of trench warfare.

became prime minister – and he floated the absurd idea of a sort of 'land-ship' in which troops and guns would somehow remain safe from machine-guns, float across no-man's-land to the enemy lines and over their trenches, and thus be able to destroy them.

Churchill must have thought to himself, 'Who knows about mud? I know: Tritton, king of agricultural machinery.' Churchill had seen a Foster's tractor crossing a large ditch, and asked Tritton whether a machine could be constructed that could cross trenches. He appointed a land-ships committee on 20 February 1915, and at the end of July sent Wilson up to meet Tritton in the White Hart, and explain what sort of vehicle he wanted.

First, the sides of the vehicle must be able to stop machine-gun bullets. Second, it should have no wheels to get bogged down in mud or ensnared by barbed wire. Third, it had to be able to get out of trenches.

On this basis Tritton got to work, and on 19 September – within thirty-seven days of the first meeting – had produced a prototype, which he called Little Willie, after himself. It had funny steering wheels at the back, which persisted into the Mark II, called Big Willie. Within a few months they had an armoured vehicle ready to tackle the machine-guns, the mud, and the trenches – a vehicle with no wheels at all.

The walls were made of half-inch steel

plate, enough to stop machine-gun bullets. There were no wheels; drive was provided by caterpillar tracks. (These were invented in 1906 by another agricultural engineer, David Roberts, for the Hornby chain tractor, but no one wanted them, so he sold the idea to the Americans, and Tritton had to buy it back again!) Perhaps Tritton's most crucial idea was the tank's extraordinary shape, with a high rising front, about 6 feet off the ground. The point was that if it did get into a trench the tank effectively had its own ramp: the front end was almost at the top of the trench already, and the tank could simply drive up, out of the trench, and away.

In the Fosters factory a secret name was needed for these new vehicles, because the enemy had to be kept in the dark. So they were officially labelled 'Water carriers for Mesopotamia'. That was a bit of a mouthful for everyday use in the factory, so the workers called them 'water tanks', and eventually just 'tanks'.

The first real Tritton tanks went into action in France on 15 September 1916 with a standard crew of seven or eight men. After a few teething troubles, they were a resounding success, and the stalemate of trench warfare was finished. Tritton was knighted in 1917, and became Sir William Tritton, but poor David Roberts received no credit at all; he died in 1928 without getting even a letter of thanks.

There is a Mk IV Tritton tank in the Museum of Lincolnshire Life in Lincoln, and various tanks at the Bovington Tank Museum, east of Dorchester, and at the Imperial War Museum in London. Close beside Lincoln's beautiful cathedral, at the top of Steep Hill, the White Hart is a pleasant and comfortable hotel, but not cheap.

30. WILLIAM PETTY AND THE CATAMARAN

Having looked at the lives of so many pioneers, it is natural to fantasise about when in history it would have been most interesting to have lived. Two periods stand out: the beginning of the industrial boom at the end of the eighteenth century, when Boulton and Watt held sway in Birmingham; and the period just after the restoration of Charles II when science was at the centre of the nation's life, Isaac Newton was around, and the Royal Society was set up. Nowhere near as famous as Newton, Hooke and the rest, William Petty was nevertheless one of the founding fellows of the Royal Society. He was an anatomist, an economist, a cartographer and a naval architect, and in 1662 in Dublin he designed and built the fastest boat in the world.

William Petty was born on 26 May 1623 in a house in Church Street, Romsey, in Hampshire. Normally this detail wouldn't be of much interest, except that by an amazing coincidence another hero lived in Church Street, Romsey, who was also a boat designer! Indeed, Edward Lyon Berthon (1813–99) was Rector of Romsey Abbey, the magnificent church for which the street is named, and which dominates the town. Berthon invented various nautical devices, most famously his folding lifeboats, and although he wrote extensively, he never seems to have mentioned the other pioneer of Church Street. Petty's father was a clothier, and though his 'principal amusement was looking on at the skilled tradesmen', at an early age William went to sea. He was such a precocious child (brat might be a better word) that his fellow seamen left him deserted on a French beach with a broken leg.

William was a resourceful chap, and instead of returning home he made enough money teaching English and navigation to enter a Jesuit College at Caen, where he received a good general education. He clearly liked learning and went on to study at Utrecht, Amsterdam and Leyden in 1644, before finally returning to Oxford to finish his medical studies. It was here that he began regular meetings in his own rooms and those of Dr Wilkins to discuss experimental natural sciences. This group was a forerunner of the Royal Society.

He soon gained fame for reviving the 'corpse' of Anne Green, who in 1650 was sentenced to be hanged for murder. The execution was carried out on the morning of 14 December. After half an hour she was cut down and pronounced dead by the sheriff. Her body, like that of any executed felon, had been promised to Petty, the young anatomist, for dissection. Fortunately he immediately realised that she was not in fact dead. He revived her with a curious combination of medical techniques, including bleeding, warming by 'a buxom lady', and the digesting of 'powdered Egyptian mummy'. Incredibly, Anne Green came back to life, was pardoned, became a bit of a celebrity and went on to have a happy family life. Petty's medical reputation was enhanced no end by this act of seemingly miraculous medicine, and he was appointed Professor of Anatomy at Brasenose College, Oxford.

His medical fame gained him the well-paid post of physician-general to Cromwell's forces in Ireland. It was here that he completely changed tack and gained fame for his 'Down Survey' of Ireland. The 1653 Act of Settlement meant that the soldiers and the army's financial backers, called 'adventurers', were to be paid with confiscated Irish land. Benjamin Worsley, the surveyor-general, was doing such a rotten job that Petty offered to do it himself, tendering to survey the entire country in thirteen months, providing accurate maps and borders, for £18,532. Instead of using skilled surveyors, he did the job using the now unemployed soldiers at a fraction of this cost, and made £9,000 for himself.

The unskilled soldiers managed this complex surveying task thanks to Petty's brilliance. He designed and had built simple instruments with which the soldiers noted the position of natural features and used the chain to measure distances. All the information was then laid on to gridded paper at a central office in Dublin by skilled cartographers. Petty's maps were used to sort out all the property wrangles of the following decades, and became the first complete and accurate map of Ireland.

In 1659 Charles II was restored and though Petty had worked for the Cromwellian army and was friendly with the Cromwell family, his great charm allowed him to remain on good terms with both sides. Indeed, far from being bitter, in 1661 Charles gave him the parishes of Kenmare, Tuosist and Bonane, and Petty became Sir William Petty. In 1662 Petty was a founding Fellow of the Royal Society (patronised by Charles) and that same year moved to Dublin. The family house was at what is now St Stephen's Green, on the site of the Shelbourne Hotel. This was where he began experimenting on his 'double-bottomed boat'.

He tackled the problem experimentally, trying out alternative shapes for the hull.

Instead of building full-size ships, he modelled them 'in small' as he put it. Petty was the first to experiment with ship design on a small scale, and his results showed that long thin hulls were faster than broad hulls. There are a number of reasons for this. First, a submerged hull has to part the water in front of it. The wider the hull, the further the water has to go around the boat and this takes energy, slowing the hull down. Also, a short hull makes short waves, and at certain speeds these waves slow the boat down. The longer the hull, the faster it can go before these waves affect its speed.

Unfortunately, his tests also showed that thin hulls were very unstable and liable to tip over. So, to get the best of speed and stability, he joined two long thin hulls with a deck, and invented the catamaran. The result was stable, fast and highly original. We know now that the Hawaiians and Polynesians had huge double-hulled boats, but no record of them appears in any seventeenth-century writings. For Petty, and the western world, this really was a first.

Petty then built a larger boat, each hull 20 feet long by 2 feet diameter. He called it *Invention*, but the locals named it *Simon & Jude*, as it was launched on the feast of St Simon and St Jude, 28 October 1662.

To prove his test results Petty organised a race in Dublin Bay, backed by the Royal Society. On Epiphany, 6 January 1663, he raced against a small collection of ships' boats and a 'black pleasure boate' and on the outward downwind leg, against the flood tide, covered the 2 miles in 'half a quarter of one hour' – a spectacular 16 knots. Though she suffered a broken rudder on the return leg, *Invention* comfortably won the silk flag of the Royal Society, inscribed 'Proemium

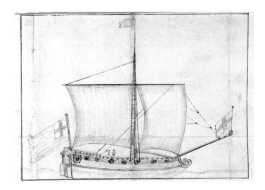

William Petty's catamaran.

Regalis Societatis Velociorum', and Petty must have thought the future was rosy for his 'double-bottomed boat'. He built bigger boats: *Experiment* was a 60-footer, carrying sixteen guns, which he sailed to Portugal and Spain, and just three years before his death he built the enormous *St Michael the Archangel*. This boat was a complete failure and Petty's hopes for catamarans disappeared with it.

Petty's main claim to fame was as a political economist – he was one of the first to analyse the nature of wealth and how nations might acquire it, realising that wealth was more to do with labour and land than gold and treasure. But when he died in 1687 he was still writing to friends, insisting that the catamaran was a winner. Although catamarans are spectacularly fast, they haven't really replaced conventional ships. However, if William Petty visited the site of that triumphant race in Dublin Bay today, he would be delighted to discover that the passengers, trucks and cars coming from Holyhead invariably travel at great speed and in any weather in a giant version of his 'double-bottomed boat'.

The high-speed ferry between Dublin and Holyhead is a catamaran, and the Shelbourne Hotel on St Stephen's Green in Dublin is on the site of Petty's house.

31. CORNELIS DREBBEL AND HIS SUBMARINE

Cornelis Drebbel was born in 1572 in Alkmaar in Holland. He started his working life as an engraver and glassworker, but his interests soon moved into alchemy and science. He published a book called *The Nature of the Elements* (i.e. earth, air, fire and water). He also ground lenses, invented a force pump for a fountain, a new type of chimney and a clockwork motor that could allegedly keep going for 100 years. He came over to England in 1604 at the request of King James I, who had heard about Drebbel's claims to have made a solar-powered perpetual motion machine.

The king gave Drebbel an income and lodgings at Eltham Palace in south-east London. In the 1400s Eltham was an important hunting lodge and country escape for the royal family, who often went there for Christmas. What's more, dignitaries from abroad, heading for London, would pop in for a wash and brush up before seeing the king. Unfortunately, in the seventeenth century the place became a ruin; all that remains now are the moat, a few walls and the magnificent great hall.

At Eltham Drebbel produced all sorts of extraordinary devices, including a compound microscope, a thermometer, a telescope, a machine that produced lightning, rain, thunder and extreme cold, a still for obtaining fresh water from salt water, wind-powered musical instruments and toys, an incubator, a thermostatically controlled oven and an extraordinary pump.

About 1620 Drebbel set about making a submarine. We have no accurate contemporary description, but it was probably like two rowing boats, the second clamped upside down on top of the first, and the whole thing covered in greased leather. There was a watertight hatch, a rudder and four oars. There were two things that were really clever about Drebbel's submarine: first, how he got it to sink and then to resurface; second, how the passengers and crew breathed under water.

His solution to the first problem was to put under the rowers' seats large pigskin bladders, connected to the outside by pipes. When the bladders were flooded, the boat would sink; when the water was squeezed out again, the submarine would surface. When the submarine set off, the bladders were empty and tied shut with rope. When the crew wanted to dive they untied the rope, allowed the bladders to fill with water, and down she went. When they wanted to surface the crew squashed the bladders flat, squeezing the water out.

Drebbel was so satisfied with his submarine that he built two more, each bigger than the last. The final model had six pairs of oars and could carry sixteen passengers; the hull was strengthened with iron bands, and even had windows. This model was demonstrated to the king and thousands of Londoners. It could apparently stay submerged for three hours and had a range of 6 miles – allegedly they rowed in three hours from Westminster to Greenwich and back, a distance of about 6 miles (which seems highly unlikely!). The submarine cruised about 15 feet below the surface, at which depth the water pressure would have been about one and a half times normal atmospheric pressure.

To stay under water for three hours, they must have had a supply of oxygen, but this is a bit of a mystery. One account claims Drebbel had tubes to the surface

Drebbel's sub is supposed to have looked like this. What is the man on the left thinking?

steames of those that went in the vessel, he would by unstoppering a vessel full of liquor, speedily restore the troubled air'. Another account, by someone who was actually there, claimed that the substance in Drebbel's flasks was a gas. If this was true, we have to believe Drebbel had jars full of oxygen in his submarine – a full 150 years before Joseph Priestley officially discovered oxygen in the 1770s! And now we step into the realms of unknown history. What we do know about Drebbel is that he was friendly with other famous alchemists of the time.

One of his friends was a man called Sendivogius. They probably met in 1619, while Drebbel was in Prague, tutoring the children of the Holy Roman Emperor. Sendivogius had come up with his Central Nitre Theory, and probably talked to Drebbel about it.

Sendivogius's theory revolved around saltpetre, or potassium nitrate. He said it was the food for life. You could feed plants with it, and if you heated it you got aerial nitre, which was food for people. He said that without this stuff 'no mortal can live, and without which nothing grows or is generated in this world'.

If we can believe that he used Sendivogius's aerial nitre, then Cornelis Drebbel was not only the first submariner, but also the first person to put oxygen gas to use. Unfortunately, alchemists were very secretive and Drebbel never told anyone what was in those jars. He died in November 1633 – in his only real source of income at the end of his life, a pub under London Bridge.

and a set of bellows to circulate the air. Another suggestion was made by Robert Boyle in 1662. He wrote that he had spoken with 'an excellent mathematician' who was still alive and had been on the submarine. According to Boyle's account Drebbel had a 'chemical liquor' that would replace that 'quintessence of air' that was able to 'cherish the vital flame residing in the heart'.

Did Cornelis Drebbel know about oxygen? If so he took his knowledge to the grave. Boyle said that 'when [Drebbel] perceived that the finer and purer part of the air was consumed by the respiration and

Nothing remains of Drebbel's submarine, but Eltham Palace is still worth a visit.

MACHINES OF THE INDUSTRIAL REVOLUTION

The industrial revolution was fuelled by the scientific renaissance of the seventeenth century, the discoveries and revelations of Galileo, Descartes, Boyle, Newton and others. By the beginning of the eighteenth century these scientific advances were being reflected in technological developments. Abraham Darby worked out how to make iron using coke rather than charcoal, which made the process commercially viable; he built his ironworks in Coalbrookdale around 1709. And once large machines could be constructed from iron, the engineers needed power to drive them – power first from the wind and from water-wheels, and then from the condensation of steam.

32. BENJAMIN WISEMAN'S WINDMILL

Windmills have been used for thousands of years to grind corn and to pump water in order to irrigate crops. Rumour has it that the idea was invented in Persia, but anyone who has felt the power of the wind must realise that in principle there must be ways of harnessing that power, so windmills were probably built long before history was recorded. Over the centuries there have been many designs of windmill, but one of the major problems they all have to tackle is how to take power from wind coming from any direction. The simplest idea is to use a vertical axis; the standard cup anemometer for measuring wind speed is like this. Whichever way the wind blows, there is always a force pushing the arms round.

A simple device much used for irrigation in Africa is made by sawing an oil-drum in half, and bolting the two halves off-set to a vertical shaft. This makes a cheap and reliable wind-pump, but is not very efficient. Technically this device is called a Slavonius rotor, and is often seen on the forecourts of garages, spinning in the wind and advertising tyres or oil.

The latest wind-farms use what look like three-bladed propellers mounted on horizontal shafts on top of high towers. These are much more efficient than the oil-drum machines, but require much higher technology. The top of the tower has to be free to turn; there has to be a mechanism for turning it to face the wind; the generator has to be at the top of the tower, and is therefore awkward to maintain; and so on. There is quite a price to pay for efficiency.

In 1783 Benjamin Wiseman Junior, a merchant of Diss in Norfolk, took out a patent on a revolutionary kind of windmill, which was like four boats sailing round in a circle. They sailed around a vertical shaft, which solved the problem of variable wind direction. Boats can easily sail downwind and across the wind; only when sailing directly into the wind is there a real problem. Therefore whatever the direction of the wind, three of the four sails will provide some turning power, and they will easily overcome the resistance of the fourth. As each mast goes round its circle, the sail fills on one side, then 'goes about, as it faces straight into the wind, then fills on the other side, grows fuller and fuller until suddenly it gybes, and the boom smacks over to the other side'. This is lovely to watch, although a sudden burst of high wind might cause major damage rather quickly.

Wiseman was concerned about winds that were too light and winds that were too strong; he covered both possibilities in his patent. Inside the mill he designed a beam to be pushed round by a horse when

Benjamin Wiseman Junior's elegant design for a vertical axis windmill.

The author experimenting with a Wiseman windmill.

33. JOHN SMEATON'S WATER-WHEELS

John Smeaton was born in 1724 at Austhorpe Lodge, of which the gatehouse still stands near the fish-and-chip shop on the ring road in Middleton, east of Leeds. As a lad Smeaton was always dreaming and building things, and at school he was called 'Fooley' Smeaton because of his obsession with mechanics.

When he was ten or twelve he went to the coal-pit at Garforth and watched men building a Newcomen steam engine – they called it a fire engine – to pump the water out of the mine. He was fascinated, asked lots of questions, and then went home and built his own little fire engine. He tried it out on his dad's goldfish pond, and rapidly pumped all the water out, which was not at all popular with either his dad or the goldfish! Later in his life he built another steam engine to pump water up the hill to Temple Newsam House.

Smeaton became involved in the building of the canals which snaked across the country in the eighteenth century; in particular, he was appointed engineer of the Calder & Hebble Navigation, which was to run through Dewsbury, Mirfield and Huddersfield. The terrain was difficult and there was great risk of flooding, but he carried out the job with triumph until it was almost done. Then there was a change of directors, and the new board decided they did not need Smeaton, and fired him. The canal was approaching completion when a terrible flood brought near-disaster, and they quickly called him back. He completed the job, and it's still in excellent condition.

the wind dropped, so that the windmill would not stop, but be driven through a ratchet arrangement, so that if there were a sudden squall the horse would not be driven round at 30 mph. And if the wind got really strong, a cunning governor system would throw a lever and lower all the sails, so the mill would stop.

We have found no record to show whether Benjamin Wiseman Junior ever built one of his windmills, nor whether he made any money from his patent. Perhaps it was too complicated to catch on – there were a great many moving parts to go wrong – but don't you wish all those modern wind-farms had mainsheets filling with wind, as suggested in 1783 by Benjamin Wiseman Junior?

All we know of Wiseman is in his 1783 patent.

The most dramatic thing Smeaton built was the Eddystone lighthouse. The Eddystone reef is a vicious rocky outcrop that rises just above the waves in the open sea 14 miles south of Plymouth. The first lighthouse there was built by Henry Winstanley in 1698, but was washed away, along with Winstanley, in the great storm of November 1703. The second lighthouse, built by John Rudyerd, was burned to the water in 1755, and Smeaton was asked to build the third, even though he had no experience of lighthouses.

We know a good deal about what he did, for he wrote a clear and detailed account of it, and his huge book is still available. Ignoring the gloomy advice of the sceptics, he decided to build the whole thing with stone. He did a series of experiments with various cements, looking for one that would work under water, and most ingenious of all he designed the entire tower like a vast three-dimensional jigsaw puzzle, with interlocking pieces. Every piece of stone was cut into a clever shape that would lock it to the next one, even without cement.

He completed his lighthouse in 1759, and it stood there for more than 120 years, until the keepers began to worry that the rock on which it stood was being undermined and washed away by the waves. So a new lighthouse was built on another rock 30 yards away – the one that still stands there today – and the top half of Smeaton's tower was taken down and re-erected as a memorial to him on Plymouth Hoe, the green headland overlooking the Sound. In fact the rock has not collapsed yet, and the bottom half – Smeaton's Stump

– is still standing on the Eddystone. Despite another hundred years of buffeting, the stone and the pointing at the bottom look as if they are only a few decades old; only at the top, where it has no protection, is the tower showing signs of decay.

One extraordinary feature of John Smeaton was his versatility. Not only did he build steam engines, canals and lighthouses, he also carried out fundamental scientific research on windmills and water-wheels. His paper to the Royal Society about windmills discussed such things as the optimum shapes and angles for the sails, while his work on water-wheels sorted out a vigorous controversy.

There are two types of water-wheel: the undershot wheel, where the water simply flows underneath and pushes the wheel round, and the overshot wheel, where the water spills into buckets on the top of the wheel and the weight of water in the buckets pushes it round. The French scientist Antoine Parent claimed that the undershot wheel was six times more efficient than the overshot, while John Theophilus Desaguliers asserted that the overshot was ten times as efficient as the undershot.

Smeaton had had several commissions to build water-wheels, and wanted to know the truth. He reckoned the only way to settle this 'monstrous disagreement' was to run some experiments. He built himself a beautiful model about 4 feet long and 5 feet high, with a water-wheel that he could arrange to drive either undershot or overshot, using water from a cistern. He designed it with various movable parts, so that he

'Smeaton's Stump' as it is today. The lighthouse remained structurally sound, but had to be dismantled when the rock underneath began to give way.

could vary the flow of water and alter the drag on the wheel.

He realised that friction was a serious problem, and most of the power available might be used in overcoming it. So he cunningly measured the frictional drag on the wheel by measuring the smallest force that would just keep it turning. Then he knew he had to add this force to any extra force doing useful work.

The paper he read to the Royal Society on 3 May 1759 is hard work to read – much more difficult than his account of building the lighthouse! – and contains sentences such as:

The area of the head being 105.8 inches, this multiplied by the weight of water of the inch cubic, equal to the decimal .579 of the ounce avoirdupoise, gives 61.26 ounces for the weight of as much water, as is contained in the head, upon 1 inch in depth, 1/16 of which is 3.83 pounds; this multiplied by the depth 21 inches, gives 80.43 lb for the value of 12 strokes; and by proportion, 39½ (the number made in a minute) will give 264.7 lb the weight of water expended in a minute.

However, his logic appears to be impeccable, and his conclusion is clear: 'The effect therefore of overshot wheels, under the same circumstances of quantity and fall, is at a medium double to that of the undershot. . .' In other words, he

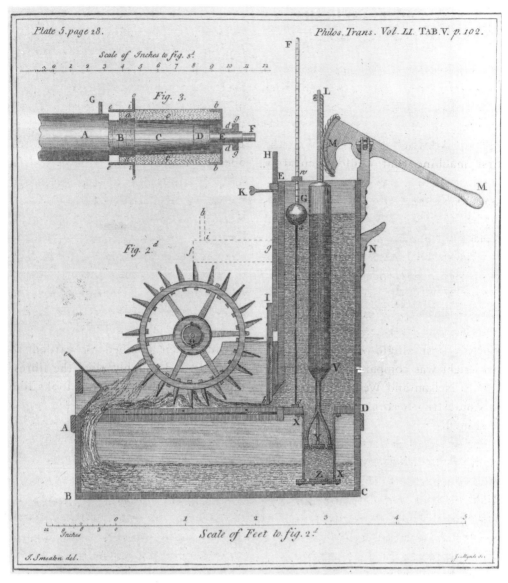

Smeaton's water-wheel.

found the overshot wheel twice as efficient as the undershot.

For his work on windmills and water-wheels the Royal Society awarded him a gold medal, and he was one of the earliest engineers to take such a scientific view of the world.

Smeaton's memorial in the church at Whitkirk, Leeds, carries a carved stone relief model of the Eddystone lighthouse. The real thing still stands, half on the reef where it was built, the top half as a tourist attraction on Plymouth Hoe. The Calder & Hebble Navigation still carries boats between Dewsbury and Huddersfield, and wherever possible millwrights have made overshot water-wheels, following Smeaton's pioneering experiments.

34. RICHARD ARKWRIGHT'S WATER-FRAME AND MILL

In this section there are plenty of candidates for the invention that powered the industrial revolution. But what would all these engines drive? Sir Richard Arkwright (1732–92) built the first machine that could accurately reproduce the actions of a skilled manual worker – but he went much further. One of his 'water-frames' could replace not one but nearly one hundred workers; and Arkwright was a businessman with the vision to see that these new machines would allow him to organise labour in more efficient ways, opening up what was probably the world's first single-purpose factory. Arkwright was compared by Sir Robert Peel to Nelson and Wellington, and yet this industrial hero had a very modest start in life.

Richard's father was a peruke or wig-maker in Preston, Lancashire, and as the youngest of thirteen children Richard was last in line for the education his brothers received. Instead he, too, was apprenticed as a hairdresser and earned a living as a wig-maker, basing himself in Bolton from about 1750. Not much is known about Arkwright's early life, but a letter about the great man's time in Bolton written in 1799 concludes: 'He was always thought to be clever in his peruke making business and very capital in Bleeding and toothdrawing and allowed by all in his acquaintance to be [a] very ingenious man.' The account may benefit from hindsight, because we know of no Arkwright inventions from this time. As well as a barber, Arkwright became publican of the Black Boy Inn.

In Bolton, as in much of Lancashire, the textile trade was growing fast, fuelled in part by new technology. The fly shuttle had been patented by John Kay in 1733, and greatly speeded up the operation of the hand-loom while making it possible for one person to operate it. This increased the demand for thread and in about 1738 Lewis Paul, son of a French refugee, invented a mechanical process which he failed to make work, but which formed the basis for Arkwright's invention. Spinning thread on a spinning wheel is a skilled manual job. The cotton (or wool) has already been combed or carded to untangle and roughly align the fibres, but to the untutored eye it looks like cotton wool. The spinster, as the female spinners were known, holds a handful of the raw cotton and lets it tease out through her fingers as it is wound on to a bobbin. So the first part of the process is teasing, which reduces the handful to the number of fibres needed in the thread. As the teased fibres are wound on to the bobbin, they are given a twist which locks the fibres together and tightens or hardens the thread. It was the finger-tip control of the spinsters that Paul and Arkwright would try to mimic, and to multiply.

The spinning wheel already inserted twist as it wound the thread. The challenge was to tease the cotton mechanically. Arkwright hit upon the same idea as Lewis Paul – roller spinning. The carded cotton is fed through two or more sets of rollers

Cromford Mill, Derbyshire, probably the first single-purpose factory in the country.

which pinch it tightly. But the second set of rollers goes faster than the first, and thus stretches or teases out the thread. Further sets of rollers can be used to tease the cotton further. But making this work in practice was another matter, and while Paul's business gradually failed, Arkwright used roller-spinning to found an empire. Arkwright teamed up with a watchmaker called John Kay (though not the man of the same name who had invented the flying shuttle). Kay was to help him build his machine, which was completed in about 1767. They had moved to Preston where Arkwright maintained the deceit that the machine was for calculating longitude. Preston is also the location for the story about 'strange noises' in the night as the men worked on the machine, forcing the neighbours to conclude that this was 'the devil tuning his bagpipes'. This seems so unlikely that it must have been made up – there are similar stories accompanying other inventions. Despite the strange noises, the men had made the machine work. In particular, Arkwright had worked out how the distances between rollers and the force with which they were squeezed together could be used to mimic the control of the skilled spinsters.

The following year Arkwright and Kay took the invention to Nottingham, then the centre of the cotton stocking trade. At about this time another invention, the famous 'Spinning Jenny', was put into operation in Nottingham by James Hargreaves. This too could produce cotton thread, but only for the 'weft', the threads that run along the length of a cloth. Arkwright's invention could produce thread for the warp as well.

The first 'spinning-frame' was driven by horses, but this proved both inconvenient and uneconomical. He had patented his invention in 1769, the year James Watt took out his master patent

spring water, and it was the same water that drew Arkwright there. Cromford was served by a warm spring that never froze even in the coldest winter. It was the ideal place for the world's first factory.

A single spinster could spin a single thread. A Spinning Jenny could produce perhaps twenty threads at a time. But in its final form Arkwright's machine, now called the 'water-frame' thanks to its new motive power, could spin ninety-six threads at the same time using just one unskilled operator. Arkwright had made cotton spinning into child's play. So, of course, he needed children to operate it.

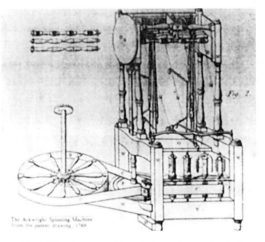

Arkwright's spinning machine: visible on top are the leather-covered rollers that tease out the cotton roving.

Arkwright's machine made spinning child's play — so of course he hired children to do the work!

for improving steam engines, and no doubt the idea of motive power for industry was in the air. Arkwright settled on water power, and teamed up with Mr Need of Nottingham and Mr Strutt of Derby, who had the patents for the manufacture of ribbed stockings, and set up his spinning-frame at Cromford in Derbyshire. The area is famed for its

He advertised for workers with large families, all of whom could be employed. Arkwright seems to have supported the idea of child labour because it took such a long time to learn the trade that if 'they were not to go until they were twelve or thirteen they would be leaving when they became useful'. He favoured a minimum age no higher then ten. But for the time, conditions at Cromford were extremely good. Decent houses were built for the mill workers, and also for the weavers and the others who supported or were fed by the water-frame. Although he used children, they were not admitted until they could read, and he made sure that there was schooling for all. Indeed it was pressure from the parents that made sure plenty of children were available. Profits from the mill were so great that it was kept working twenty-three hours a day, with an hour for oiling and cleaning the machines.

Arkwright's thread was better than any cotton thread then available in Britain. The only full cotton fabric had come from India, the locally produced cloth being a mixture of cotton and flax because the British cotton thread was not hard enough. This caused an anomaly because cotton cloth was subject to duty, supposedly because it was imported. An Act of Parliament put the matter right and allowed Arkwright to reap the rewards of his invention. His empire expanded into mills all over the country.

He also sold and licensed the machines to others, raking in a vast income for himself but stoking up resentment at his stranglehold on the industry. There were many attempts to use the technology – both the water-frame and later a very successful carding machine – without paying the inventor. The matter came to a head in a series of trials in which Arkwright attempted to prosecute those who had tried to 'steal' his patented machines – but the result was not as he had hoped. In 1781 before the King's Bench,

Arkwright's case against Charles Lewis Mordaunt was heard before Lord Mansfield. Surprisingly, Mordaunt did not deny that he had infringed the patent. Rather, he argued, the patent itself was not valid. The court found in Mordaunt's favour, agreeing that Arkwright had not fully revealed the specification as a patentee is required to do, but 'did all he could to hide and secrete it'. In the subsequent trial of 1785, it was suggested that the invention was not new, having been secretly stolen and passed to Arkwright by John Kay, the man who helped him build the prototype spinning machine. James Watt himself had been called as a witness and wrote, 'Though I do not love Arkwright, I don't like the precedent of setting aside patents . . . I fear for our own.'

Despite the loss of his patents, it is difficult to feel sorry for Sir Richard Arkwright. The invention was merely the starting point for the real revolution – the organisation of mills along factory lines. Arkwright was so brilliant a businessman that by the time he died in 1792 he had amassed £500,000, worth perhaps £200 million today. There is a wonderful description of the great man by Carlyle: 'A plain, almost gross, bag-cheeked, potbellied Lancashire man, with the air of painful reflection, yet also of copious free digestion.' Not a conventional hero, then, but he changed the face of British industry.

The mill at Cromford in Derbyshire is being restored, and is open to the public. There is an original water-frame in the Helmshore Textile Museum in Rossendale (01706 226459).

35. EDMUND CARTWRIGHT AND HIS POWER LOOM

The sleepy farming village of Goadby Marwood, a few miles north of Melton Mowbray in Leicestershire, does not look like a hotbed of technology, but Edmund Cartwright, inventor extraordinary, was the rector there from 1779 until 1786. He fancied himself as a poet and he invented a great variety of things from interlocking bricks to a cure for putrid fever, but he's best known for the power loom, patented in 1785.

Edmund Cartwright was born on 24 April 1743 at Marnham in Nottinghamshire. He went to Wakefield Grammar School and was sent off to Oxford to study for the Church. While he was at Oxford he published a long poem called *Armina and Elvira*, which was praised by Sir Walter Scott and others, and went through several editions. On the strength of this one good poem and a few mediocre others, he later called himself 'The Father of Poetry' – which seems more than a little presumptuous – and declared that all later poets were his children!

In 1784 Cartwright went up to Derbyshire on holiday, and visited Richard Arkwright and his amazing cotton spinning mill at Cromford. In 1769 Arkwright had patented the water-frame, and his mill was one of the first mass-production factories in the world. After seeing the Cromford mill, Cartwright went to a pub in Matlock and got chatting to some cotton men from Manchester; they reckoned that if a few more mills like Arkwright's were built, there would be more cotton thread than the weavers could cope with, and the spinners would have to start exporting the thread. Cartwright said 'Well, Mr Arkwright should invent a weaving machine, too.'

The others dismissed this as impossible, but Cartwright, who had heard about an automaton chess-player being exhibited in London, said if you could build a machine to play chess you could surely build a machine to weave cloth. In fact the chess-playing automaton, known as 'The Turk', was a conjuring trick. Built in Vienna in 1769 by the Hungarian engineer Baron Wolfgang von Kempelen, it created tremendous excitement when it took on all comers and won, moving the pieces with its left hand. The doors of the chest were opened before the performance, and the inside seemed to be full of intricate machinery, but in fact hidden inside was a very small, very skilful chess player, with a large bladder.

Not knowing it was a fake, Cartwright went home to Goadby Marwood and set about building a weaving machine! He had never seen anyone weaving, and had no idea how it was done, but he wandered about the house making shuttle movements with his hands, which sent his children into fits of giggles, and in the end he managed to construct a power loom, which he patented in April 1785. His patent and the drawing are exceedingly vague; you can tell he'd never seen a loom before. His machine wasn't a great success – two burly men were needed to make it work

NOW KNOW YE, that I, the said Edmund Cartwright, in pursuance of and in compliance with the said proviso in the said recited Royal Letters 5 Patent contained, do, by this present Instrument, hereby declare that the nature of my said New-invented Machine for Weaving, and the manner in which the same is to be performed (is as follows) :—

It is worked by a mechanical force. The warp, instead of lying horizontally, as in the common looms, is in this machine (which may be made to hold any 10 number of webs at pleasure) placed perpendicularly. The shuttle, instead of being thrown by hand, is thrown either by a spring, the vibration of a pendulum, the stroke of a hammer, or by the application of one of the mechanical powers, according to the nature of the work and the distance the shuttle is required to be thrown. And lastly, the web winds up gradually as it is woven. 15 And for the better illustration of my said New-invented Weaving Machine, the same is more particularly described and ascertained in the Plan or Drawing hereunto annext.

In witness whereof, I, the said Edmund Cartwright, have hereunto set my hand and seal, this Twenty-eighth day of April, in the twenty-20 fifth year of the reign of our Sovereign Lord King George the Third, by the grace of God, of Great Britain, France, and Ireland, Defender of the Faith, and so forth, and so forth, and in the year of our Lord One thousand seven hundred and eighty-five.

EDMUND (L.S.) CARTWRIGHT.

Part of Cartwright's 1785 patent for his power loom.

– so Cartwright set about improving the design.

First he went to see a weaver, and was amazed by the simplicity of the process, which had scarcely changed in centuries, apart from John Kay's invention of the flying shuttle in 1733. This allowed the weaver to throw the bobbin of weft thread from one side of the warp to the other with one hand, and more than doubled the rate of weaving.

Basically cloth is woven by passing one thread, the weft, backwards and forwards between the long warp threads that run from one end of the cloth to the other, and comprises three actions: shedding, picking and beat-up. Shedding is the making of a tunnel or shed between the warp threads for the weft to pass through. Picking is passing or throwing the weft through the shed. Beat-up is pressing the new weft thread down against the previous one to form a

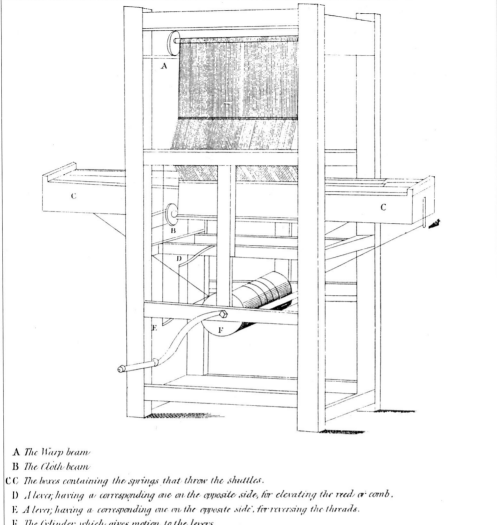

A *The Warp beam*
B *The Cloth beam*
CC *The boxes containing the springs that throw the shuttles.*
D *A lever; having a corresponding one on the opposite side, for elevating the reed or comb.*
E *A lever; having a corresponding one on the opposite side, for reversing the threads.*
F *The Cylinder, which gives motion to the levers.*
   N.B. The warp is kept to a due degree of tension by the counteraction of either a weight or spring.
The web is made to wind by the like power, tho'   in an inferior degree, and is prevented, as the stroke of the
reed or comb brings it down from unwinding by a ratch wheel and click.

The vague diagram in Cartwright's patent.

new edge on the cloth being woven. Until Cartwright's day these three actions were done by hand, and a good weaver could do perhaps 100 picks a minute.

Cartwright's second machine made all the actions automatic, and therefore enabled them to be much faster. Even a pedal-powered loom enabled a competent weaver to do 160 picks a minute. But clearly there was potential for using external power; Cartwright had been much impressed with Arkwright's water-powered spinning. He set up a weaving factory in Doncaster, powered initially by a water-wheel, and in April 1789 gave a dinner to his workforce of 120 people. They had a whole roast sheep, several pieces of beef, and about thirty plum puddings, and they drank at least eight toasts, so it must have been a good party.

But Cartwright wanted to go further. He planned to use a steam engine to drive his looms, and that's when he began to hit trouble. Thousands of weavers could see their jobs disappearing, and they took drastic action. Grimshaws set up a factory in Manchester, and planned to put in 400 looms, but received threatening letters: 'Sir, we have sworn together to destroy your factory, if we die for it, and to have your life for ruining our trade. . .' And when only twenty-four looms had been installed, the factory was burned to the ground. No one else dared try such an experiment.

Cartwright's loom was one of the major innovations of the industrial revolution, and in 1789 he patented a wool-combing machine that could do the work of at least twenty men. But again the workers protested; into the House of Commons poured petitions against its use from 50,000 wool-combers. After two great inventions Cartwright hadn't made a penny, but to his credit he kept on inventing.

In 1795 he patented interlocking bricks. He was worried about the fact that houses were built with timber supports, and were liable to catch fire, and he was trying to build fire-proof houses. His bricks were intended to make timber supports unnecessary. He made simple bricks for making a normal wall, and more intricate ones for building self-supporting arches and domes. They simply plugged together like pieces of a jigsaw puzzle – and indeed like the stones of John Smeaton's Eddystone lighthouse. Unfortunately, although these bricks were a brilliant idea, they were too expensive to be popular, and never caught on.

In 1806, Cartwright's last loom patent expired and rivals were free to make power looms without paying Cartwright a penny. So in 1807 a group of Manchester businessmen went to the prime minister and asked for money, on the grounds that Cartwright had spent £30,000 of his own money on inventions that were good for the country, but had made no money from them. In 1809 the government gave him £10,000!

He took the money, retired to a farm in Sussex, and continued inventing things that nobody would ever use. In 1823 he thought up an engine fired by gunpowder. Luckily, he died peacefully before he had the chance to blow himself up. He left behind countless useless inventions and one which made his name – the power loom.

Goadby Marwood is a lovely village, and well worth a visit, although there are no signs of Cartwright's incumbency, apart from a list in the church. The looms at the Bradford Industrial Museum show at a glance the extraordinary development of looms brought about by the self-appointed 'Father of Poetry'.

36. THOMAS SAVERY'S PATENT FOR RAISING WATER BY FIRE

The industrial revolution changed the world for ever. Some would argue that the intellectual drive may have come from the Lunar Society in Birmingham; certainly the idea of gathering a large workforce in a single factory was perhaps started by Richard Arkwright in Derbyshire; but what gave the whole thing momentum was the harnessing of power, and in particular the power of steam.

Most people think the steam engine was invented by James Watt, but in fact the first practical machine was patented forty years before Watt was born – in fact, in the year that James Watt's father was born – 1698. What's more, that machine was invented not in London, nor in Manchester, nor in Birmingham, but at Shilston Barton in South Devon, by Thomas Savery.

Thomas was born about 1650 into a wealthy family. They bought a medieval manor house and built on a huge extension. As the younger son of a younger son, Thomas was a gent, but had no land to work, so he devoted his mind to engineering and invention. In 1696 he patented both a machine for polishing glass and marble and another for 'Rowing of ships with greater ease and expedicion then hath hitherto beene done by any other'. This seems to have been a capstan attached to paddle-wheels – a sort of seventeenth-century pedalo. In those days all patents were issued by the king. Luckily Savery knew

William III – William of Orange – and William liked his rowing machine, so Savery got a patent – but the navy turned it down, which made him really cross.

He seems to have been a military engineer, and he must have known about all the mines being worked nearby, especially the tin mines in Cornwall. The miners had a real problem. The surface seams had been worked out, and when the miners dug down, the mines filled up with water. To begin with they baled it out by hand, then they used horses, but deep mines were difficult to keep from flooding.

One evening after dinner, so the story goes, Savery threw his wine bottle on the fire, observed the last of the wine inside turning into steam, and in a flash of brilliance realised the steam must be pushing the air out of the bottle. He grabbed the bottle, and thrust the neck into a bowl of water. The steam inside condensed, the water slowly rose up into the bottle, and Savery reckoned that if a wine bottle could pull water up out of a bowl, then a bigger bottle could pull water up out of a mine.

So he made himself a model, showed it to the king, and got himself another patent – for 'raiseing water by the impellant force of fire'. He also demonstrated his machine to the Royal Society on 14 June 1699. The patent has no diagram, nor even a description of the engine, but in 1702 he published a book called *The Miners Friend; or, an Engine to raise Water by Fire, Described. And of the manner of Fixing it in Mines. With an Account of the several other Uses it is*

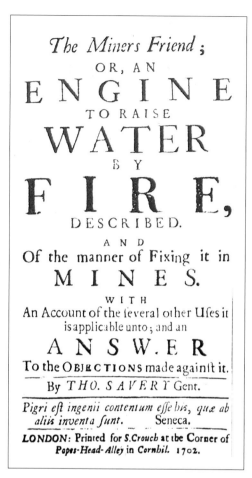

The Miners Friend, Savery's book describing his engine to raise water by fire, dedicated rather crawlingly to the king.

Light the Fire at B. When the water in N boils, the Handle of the Regulator mark'd Z must be thrust from you as far as twill go, which makes all the steam rising from the water in L pass with irresistible Force through O into P, pushing out the Air before it, through the Clack R making a noise as it goes. And when all is gone out, the Bottom of the Vessel P will be very hot.

In his book, Savery describes vividly what happened when the machine worked:

> On the outside of the vessel you may see how the water goes out, as if the vessel were transparent. For as the steam continues within the vessel, so far is the vessel dry without, and so very hot as scarce to endure the least touch of the hand. But as far as the water is, the said vessel will be cold and wet, where any water has fallen on it; which cold and moisture vanishes as fast as the steam, in its descent, takes place of the water.

applicable unto; and an Answer to the Objections made against it.

The book is a wonderful mixture. First, there's a crawling letter to the king, in very large print – perhaps he was worried that the King had poor eyesight, then one to the Royal Society, and a ten-page sales pitch to the Gentlemen Adventurers in the Mines of England. Then follows a diagram and detailed instructions – just as you might get for a video machine today. First installation, then operation; for example, page 15:

He was at pains to say how powerful his engine was, and he actually invented the term 'horse-power' – deliberately making it rather more than most horses could manage so that his customers would not be disappointed.

A few Savery' engines were probably used in mines. One was installed to control the water supply at Hampton Court. Another at Campden House in Kensington was still running eighteen years later. But they were not robust. The water was pushed out by positive steam

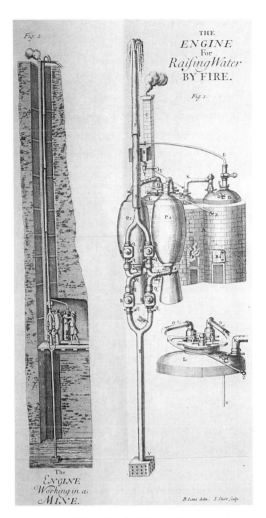

Savery suggested his engine should be installed near the bottom of the mineshaft.

pressure, and that needed high-pressure steam. The solder and the joints could not take the pressure, and as a result the machines kept going wrong. However, the Savery engine was the first practical use of steam power, and under Captain Savery's patent the steam engine came of age.

Shilston Barton is a private house. There appear to be no remaining Savery engines. However, modern copies of The Miner's Friend *appear from time to time.*

37. THOMAS NEWCOMEN AND THE FIRST WORKING STEAM ENGINES

Dartmouth, dominated by the Royal Naval College on the hill, has always been a seafaring town, made rich by traders from the sixteenth century onwards, and I wasn't surprised to learn that in 1749 Nathaniel Symons of Harberton tested his diving machine in the River Dart and, according to the *Gentlemen's Magazine*, was lucky enough to come up again in 45 minutes; nor that in 1875 William Froude made a small steam engine there to use on steam yachts. But I *was* surprised to find that within a hundred yards of the quayside Thomas Newcomen invented and developed the first steam engine that really drained the mines. Indeed Thomas Newcomen, arguably the most inventive practical genius of all time, was born in 1663 right on the quayside.

He may have been apprenticed in Exeter, but it seems he went back to Dartmouth about 1685 and set up as an ironmonger, with John Calley, who was a plumber, as his assistant. In 1707 Newcomen rented a big house between Higher and Lower Streets. Unfortunately, the whole row of houses was pulled down in 1864 in order to join Southtown with the rest of Dartmouth. But at least the new road that forms the connection is called Newcomen Road.

Thomas Newcomen called himself an ironmonger, but in fact he was more like what we would call a blacksmith; he made tools for people. He probably visited mines and made tools for the miners, so he would have known about the problems of flooding. He realised that there would be a great future for anyone

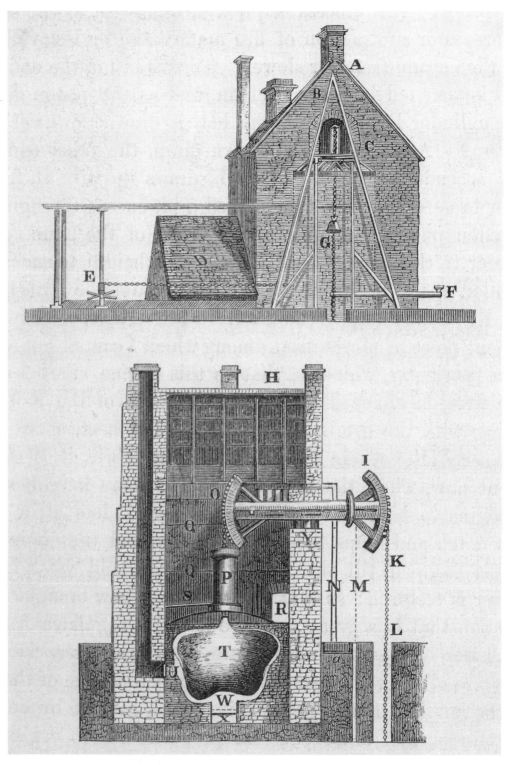

How the engine would have been installed above a mine. The incredibly deep Cornish mines sometimes needed pump rods 2,000 feet long, a tremendous load for the engine. T is the boiler, P the working cylinder and L the chain attached to the top of the pump rods.

who could make a machine to drain the mines, and that was what he did.

Like Savery, he condensed steam to make a vacuum, but whereas Savery had simply used that vacuum to pull the water up, Newcomen made his vacuum inside a cylinder, and used it to pull down a piston. Then a big lever transferred the force to the pump shaft which went down the mine.

Newcomen's engine was the first practical engine to use a piston in a cylinder. Casting the cylinders and getting the pistons to fit was just at the limit of existing technology, and the technique was generally to make the piston deliberately smaller than the cylinder by an inch or two, and to make a seal of wet leather or wet rope to close the gap. We have no idea how long Newcomen spent developing his engine, nor how many prototypes he built, although some rumours say the first effective one was built at Wheal Vor mine in Cornwall, but the first working engine of which there is good evidence was installed at a coal mine at Dudley Castle in 1712, twenty-four years before James Watt was born. That engine's cylinder was 21 inches in diameter and nearly 8 feet long, and it worked at the sedate pace of twelve strokes a minute, raising 10 gallons of water from a depth of 156 feet, which corresponds to about 5½ horse-power.

Newcomen engines worked day and night, as long as there was enough coal. They were less than 1 per cent efficient, and used a lot of coal, which was why they were installed first in coal mines where coal was free. But they were rugged and reliable.

Gradually the technology improved and they could be made with bigger cylinders, up to 6 feet in diameter. The one at Fresnes in France replaced a plant worked

Wheal Vor mine, possibly the site of Newcomen's first engine. The characteristic shape of these great engine houses still punctuates the skyline in this part of Cornwall.

by twenty men and fifty horses. By the time Thomas Newcomen died in 1729 at least a hundred of his engines were working all over Britain, and also in France, Belgium, Holland, Sweden, Hungary, Germany, and Austria. They were manufactured for more than a hundred years. The Pentich engine was still working 127 years after installation – rather different from the engines we buy in cars today. A Newcomen engine was used in Barnsley until 1934.

In 1714 a Newcomen engine cost about £1,000. Most people couldn't afford this much, and one chap who tried said,

> That cursed engine pumped my pockets dry
> And left no fire to warm my fingers by!

The standard deal was to rent an engine for £7 a week – which is 35 per cent: a good rate of return for the manufacturer. But Newcomen didn't get rich. Savery's patent, which by the Fire Engine Act of 1698 had been extended until 1733, covered all engines that raised water by fire, and said:

> if any person or persons . . . shall at any time . . . presume to make, imitate, use, or exercise any vessells or engines for raiseing water or occasioning motion to any sort of millwork by the impellant force of fire, he or they shall forfeite to the said Thomas Savery . . . all and every such vessells and engines . . .

So Newcomen was forced to go into partnership with Savery, and seems never to have made much from his fantastic invention, although Savery did give him some shares. What's worse, the scientific establishment would not believe that a provincial ironmonger could have invented such an amazing machine, so Newcomen got no scientific credit at all. They said he had pinched other people's ideas and made advances by sheer luck. Whatever the establishment view, working out how to raise water by fire was one of the greatest technological advances of all time, made in the early years of the eighteenth century by Thomas Newcomen, ironmonger, of Dartmouth.

The Cornish countryside is studded with derelict engine houses, especially around Camborne and Redruth. In Dartmouth Newcomen's house was demolished, but Newcomen Road runs up the hill where the house was, and has a small plaque on the wall. There's an attractive brass plaque on a slab of stone in the memorial gardens on the quayside, and in the back of the tourist information office is a genuine Newcomen Engine, which was bought second-hand in 1821 and used to pump water into the Coventry Canal; it can be made to run with an electric motor. A steam-powered modern replica of the original Dudley engine is on display at the Black Country Museum in Dudley, and runs occasionally (0121 557 9643).

38. JAMES WATT'S IMPROVEMENTS AND DOUBTS

James Watt is incredibly famous – but for all the wrong things. He had a brilliant mind and came up with some stunning ideas, but he would never have completed anything useful if he had not been controlled and driven by tycoon Matthew Boulton. Most people think James Watt invented the steam engine, but that is completely wrong; Newcomen engines were pumping water from mines all over the country by the time James was born on 19 January 1736.

James Watt was born in Greenock on the Clyde, the son of a prosperous carpenter. He was a sickly lad, and constantly ill. Four elder brothers and one sister all died in infancy, and his younger brother and sister also died young. James grew up expecting poor health, suffered recurring migraines, and was a lifelong hypochondriac, and yet he lived to be eighty-three!

In 1763, while working as an assistant instrument-maker in Glasgow University, Watt was brought a model Newcomen engine, which had just been repaired, and was asked to get it working. He managed to get it running, but only just; the engine was highly inefficient. In May 1765, while he was walking on a Sunday afternoon in the Green of Glasgow, he had a vision of how to make the Newcomen engine more efficient by using a separate condenser. Within a few hundred yards he had the whole thing worked out: as he put it, 'I had not walked further than the golf-house when the whole thing was arranged in my mind.'

The drawback of the Newcomen

engine was that when the cylinder was full of steam, the whole cylinder had to be cooled with cold water in order to get the steam to recondense for the power stroke. Then the whole cylinder had to be heated up again before it would fill with steam. An enormous amount of heat was being wasted. Watt talked this over with his friend Joseph Black at the university, and Black explained his new ideas about latent heat, which he had worked out for the whisky distillers. Even when you have water at 100°, you need a lot of extra heat – latent heat – to turn it into steam. That latent heat is half the cost of making whisky, and was the heat being wasted in the Newcomen engine.

Watt's idea was to keep the working cylinder hot, but to connect it to a cold container – the condenser. When the cylinder was full of steam, the tap was opened to this second container, and all the steam condensed in there. Then the tap was closed, and the cylinder was ready to fill with steam. Because it was still hot, little steam was wasted. This made a huge difference. In 1768 Watt applied for his first patent, which basically specified three things: that the working cylinder was to be kept hot, that the steam was to be condensed in a separate container; and that he intended 'in many cases to employ the expansive force of steam to press on the pistons' (although in practice he never did this; it was left to Trevithick to make high-pressure steam engines).

Almost as important to his career as that patent was his meeting with Matthew Boulton for the first time. They took an instant liking to one another. Boulton was

a forceful Birmingham businessman, a tycoon with energy and vision, exactly the opposite of Watt. It was Boulton who turned Watt from a dreamer into a Hero. But it took some years. First, Watt went off and dug the Monkland Canal. He was consulted and praised by John Smeaton, John Rennie and Thomas Telford, and yet he thought he was useless, and hated dealing with people and arguing about money.

Watt was always short of financial backing, and to feed his family he kept having to go off and survey canals and design bridges, which unfortunately was rottenly paid. In 1770 the magistrates of Hamilton wanted a new bridge over the Clyde, and asked John Smeaton if he would design it. He said he would charge a fee of £10. 'Far too much,' they said and hired Watt, who did it for 7 guineas!

Then in 1773 his Scottish backer Dr Roebuck went bankrupt, and his wife died, and James Watt finally took the plunge and moved to Birmingham, where he went into partnership with Matthew Boulton at the Soho Works. Boulton provided him with the most skilled craftsmen he could find, and enough money and time to work on the engine, and tried to keep Watt's mind fixed firmly on it. Watt had made a small engine that nearly worked in a workshop by the stream behind Dr Roebuck's house, Kinneil, at Bo'ness on the Firth of Forth, but it took him ten years to get a full-size engine running – and that was with the drive and avuncular assistance of Matthew Boulton. Watt kept going off after other hare-brained schemes, but Boulton

Watt's fee for designing Hamilton Bridge was just £7.35!

eventually persuaded him that, once his engines worked, they could make money by selling them to the owners of mines in Cornwall.

The major technical difficulty was to make a steam-tight piston-and-cylinder combination. Newcomen engines were run with perhaps an inch clearance all the

'Watt's cottage' at Kinneil House, where he built his first engine.

way round the piston, with rope or leather wound round the outside and a couple of inches of water on top. But Watt's engine needed an airtight fit, and no one could make cylinders that were truly cylindrical. Before 1775 all cylinders had been cast, the small ones from brass and the big ones from iron, but they were far from perfectly shaped.

Making the piston airtight in an imperfect cylinder was a dreadful problem. Watt tried everything he could think of, including pasteboard baked with linseed oil, papier maché, and even horse and cow dung. Nothing worked. Oil seals were hopeless, because the oil emulsified in the steam and turned into a white cream.

In the end he realised he had to get an accurately bored cylinder. He went to John 'Iron-mad' Wilkinson, who had just invented a new boring machine designed to make cannons. This machine made it possible, for the first time ever, to produce a cylinder that was both circular in cross-section and parallel throughout its length. Wilkinson delivered the first cylinder to Soho in April 1775, and within weeks Watt got his engine going, just ten years after he had had the idea. Immediately Boulton persuaded him to design two much bigger engines, of which the first was a 38 inch blowing engine for John Wilkinson's blast furnace, and the second a 50 inch pumping engine for Bloomfield Colliery near Tipton. When this was started, in March 1776, it produced a dazzling report in the local press, which said it used only a quarter of the fuel of a common (i.e. Newcomen) engine.

For twenty years John Wilkinson made all the cylinders for the Boulton and Watt engines, until they began to make their own in the Soho Foundry. Boulton and Watt supplied each customer with plans, and nominated the suppliers, but the customer ordered all the parts and paid the engine builders, including the chief erector, who was usually a Soho employee. Then, for twenty-five years, the customer paid Boulton and Watt a royalty of one-third of the coal they saved relative to a Newcomen engine of the same power. This was not too popular with the colliery owners of the Midlands, but was wonderful for Cornwall, where coal was expensive. Within a dozen years, fifty-five Boulton and Watt engines were up and running in Cornish mines.

Then Boulton persuaded Watt to make a double-acting engine, with working strokes in both directions, because he foresaw the need for rotational motion.

To convert reciprocal motion of the pistons into rotational motion of a wheel or axle, the most obvious connection was the crank, which was well known, and yet when James Watt first used a steam engine to generate rotational motion he perversely refused to use a crank! Unfortunately, in 1780 James Pickard, button-maker of Birmingham, took out a patent for an engine that included a crank. Watt was furious, and claimed that his ideas had been stolen. He threatened to sue. He also said the crank was an old idea, and could not be patented! However, he then applied for patents for five different mechanisms in order to convert reciprocal to rotary motion, including the sun-and-planet system. The sun-and-planet is all right, but it's much more complicated than just a simple crank. Nevertheless, Watt would not use another crank until Pickard's patent had expired.

Watt's double-acting engine was his most successful development, and it led him to his finest idea – parallel motion. As he told his son, many years later, 'I am more proud of the parallel motion than of any other mechanical invention I have ever made.' The problem is that the piston goes vertically up and down, and it has to push and pull an overhead beam, because to begin with that is what the engines were – beam engines. The beam pivots about its centre; so its end doesn't go vertically up and down, and if you try to connect the end of the piston directly to the beam you either get a lot of leaks, or you break the piston rod.

But make another half-beam of the same length, connect the ends with a rod, and connect your piston rod to the middle of this rod, and the problem is solved. Wherever the beam moves, this mid-point will always move in a straight line up and down. And this Watt parallel linkage was used in every sort of engine for at least 100 years. Indeed it's still occasionally used today.

James Watt was a genius: often miserable, stubborn, and resistant to change, but absolutely brilliant. He refused to use high-pressure steam, and delayed the further development of the steam engine by at least twenty years. He and Boulton would not allow their colleague William Murdock to develop either the steam carriage or gas lighting. Yet Watt invented a copying machine, sun-and-planet gears, and this wonderful parallel motion, and Boulton and Watt steam engines were the best in the world until Trevithick arrived on the scene in 1800, when Watt's patent ran out.

There's a Boulton and Watt steam engine in the Science Museum in London and a working one at the Kew Bridge Steam Museum, Green Dragon Lane, Brentford, Middlesex TW8 0EN (0181 568-4747). Watt's name is remembered in the units of power – watts and kilowatts.

39. MATTHEW MURRAY AND HIS RACK RAILWAY

'This was the first instance of the regular employment of locomotives for commercial purposes' runs a line almost casually inserted in the *Dictionary of National Biography* entry for Matthew Murray. This comes as a bit of a shock because Murray does not feature in the usual list of railway firsts. His clearly wasn't the first locomotive – that honour goes to Richard Trevithick, whose Penydaren loco ran in 1804. Before that William Murdock had built

a miniature high-pressure steam carriage perhaps as early as 1784. Yet most of us were brought up thinking that Stephenson's *Rocket* was the first proper loco to run commercially following its victory in the famous Raines Hill trial of 1829. So where does Matthew Murray fit in?

Murray (1765–1826) was born near Newcastle upon Tyne and was originally apprenticed as a blacksmith. In search of work when his indentures ended, he walked to Leeds, already a centre of the textile trade. He found work with Marshall's, famous as flax spinners. In the days before mechanised cotton-spinning, much of the cloth made in England was flax (linen) or a mixture of flax and cotton, in part because we couldn't produce hard enough cotton thread and also because imported cotton was expensive.

Nevertheless, mechanisation was becoming important and Murray proved to be a brilliant innovator. While at Marshall's he invented and patented several machines for spinning, carding and other stages in the preparation of cloth. He left in 1795 to set up on his own as Fenton, Murray, & Wood. They made flax machinery as before, but he began to spend more time on steam engines – presumably huge stationary engines of the Watt type, which would have been around for over twenty years. Murray's works was called the Round Foundry and was organised so that all the machines could take power from a central shaft powered by a vast steam engine. He turned out to be rather good at engine-building – so good that he was regarded as a serious rival by the greatest engine builders of all, Boulton and Watt

If you think Matthew looks tough, you should have seen Mrs Murray.

in Birmingham. To prevent Murray expanding, they quietly bought up all the land surrounding the Round Foundry!

This was the time of the Napoleonic wars, and the people of England were beginning to be hit quite hard. One example of the economic impact of war was the fact that horse-feed had become very expensive. A local businessman, Charles Branding, had begun to feel the pinch and wondered if it might be possible to do away with the horses altogether. He ran a coal mine up on Hunslet Moor – where the M1 motorway now leaves Leeds – and needed to transport the coal back into town. He operated a horse-drawn railway. These old railways had been around for years, and sometimes had wooden rails for trucks to run on. In other parts of the country cunning gravity-assisted systems used full trucks running downhill to pull the empties back up to the top. Branding turned to his manager, John Blenkinsop, who turned to Matthew Murray.

Blenkinsop planned to use cast-iron rails, and wondered whether Murray could build a locomotive to haul a wagon train along them. They realised that the materials available presented a serious problem. When a locomotive runs on smooth rails, it depends upon friction to get a grip. Indeed the pulling force of the locomotive is limited by friction – there comes a point where, no matter how powerful the engine, the friction is not great enough and instead of pulling the train, it spins the wheels. There is a simple way of increasing friction and thereby grip: increase the weight of the locomotive. And this is where Blenkinsop

and Murray came unstuck: their cast-iron rails would crack if the locomotive weighed more than 5 tons. A 5-ton loco could haul only 20 tons of coal. Blenkinsop eventually solved the problem by laying a third, toothed rail. A cog on the engine engaged with this 'rack' to provide drive for the train, and so got round the problem of friction. Interestingly the limits of cast-iron rails cost Richard Trevithick dearly during trials of his machine. Because his 1804 locomotive broke the rails on its way out, he was unable to complete the return journey by rail and thus lost an enormous bet!

Blenkinsop and Murray did rather better. The *Salamanca* and the *Prince Regent* were put into service in 1811, with the *Lord Wellington* and the

The Murray/Blenkinsop locomotive – you can clearly see the central toothed wheel, the key to its success on the weak rails of the day.

Marquis Wellington in the following year. This was the first commercial steam railway, four years before George Stephenson built his first locomotive. The rack technology worked extremely well. Instead of the 20 tons expected of a 5-ton locomotive, these power-houses were able to haul 90 tons. On one occasion they hauled thirty wagons at 3¼ miles an hour, an event of such note that it was witnessed by the Grand Duke Nicholas of Russia. We don't know if he was an early trainspotter, or simply didn't have anything better to do that afternoon. Murray's engines were also used in ships. Following consultations with the American ambassador in Liverpool in 1815, Murray supplied an order for the first paddle-steamer on the Mississippi!

Murray became a steam enthusiast, steam-heating his house and naming it 'Steam Hall'. Not everyone was as keen, and a group of Luddites visited the hall with crowbars one night, only to run into the formidable Mrs Murray, who saw them off with a brace of pistols. The railway ran for over twenty years, by which time materials had improved enough for cheaper, smooth rails to become standard. However, in the steep mountains of Switzerland, on Snowdon and even during construction of the Channel Tunnel, there is still a need for the rack railway, and locomotives for all these places have been built in Leeds by the Hunslet Engine Company – successors to Matthew Murray and John Blenkinsop.

The Middleton railway runs with steam trains in Matthew Murray's tracks.

40. ROBERT STIRLING'S ENGINE

This story is a bit of a mystery. Robert Stirling was the minister at Galston parish church, near Kilmarnock, for fifty-eight years. He was a Doctor of Divinity, and he devoted his life to his parishioners – there's a memorial in the church that says so. Yet in 1816, more than ten years before Stephenson's *Rocket* was made and sixty-two years before the internal combustion engine was invented, he patented an entirely new type of engine, an engine that could run on any fuel, required little maintenance, and was safe and efficient. The mystery – indeed the double mystery – is why it didn't catch on, and how a full-time minister of the Church came to make such a staggering advance in engineering science.

Robert Stirling was born at Methven near Perth, and at the age of fifteen went to Edinburgh University, where he studied Latin, Greek, logic and mathematics, before moving to Glasgow to study Divinity; he eventually became a minister in 1816. He filed his first patent just eight days after being ordained, so the engine must have been important to him.

In that first patent he mentions a device that became known as 'the economiser', and the introduction describes vaguely 'improvements for diminishing the consumption of fuel'. He says the economiser is a device for moving heat between one part of a body of gas and another; this does not sound thrilling, and you wouldn't know he was talking about a heat engine unless you had read the whole thing.

But what he proposed was very simple

The Revd Robert Stirling. It is a mystery how a dedicated and popular minister with no real engineering background came to invent and perfect such an original machine.

A.D. 1816 . . . . N° 4081.

Steam Engine and Saving Fuel.

LETTERS PATENT to Robert Stirling, of Edinburgh, Clerk, for his invented " Improvements for Diminishing the Consumption of Fuel, and in particular an Engine capable of being applied to the moving Machinery on a Principle entirely new." 6 months.

Dated 16th November 1816.

(No Specification enrolled.)

Fuel economy interested Stirling when he invented his engine 'on a principle entirely new' — but the ready supply and low cost of coal meant that it is only recently that the Stirling engine has been seriously considered as a 'prime mover'.

– and revolutionary. He realised that when you heat air, it expands. Could you, he wondered, use that expansion to do work? Well, to make it into an engine, you'd have to make it cycle somehow, which presumably meant heating up a whole cylinder, and then cooling it down again (like the Newcomen engine). Then he had a brilliant idea. Rather than heating and cooling the whole cylinder, wasting energy each time, suppose you had one end of the cylinder hot, and the other end cold; you could simply move the air from one end to the other, so it would very quickly heat and cool, expand and contract.

Stirling used two cylinders: one was the working cylinder, just like the cylinder of any engine, where the piston goes in and out and drives a flywheel through a crank. The interesting part is the displacer. This is another cylinder, connected to the first by a tube, with a lightweight piston in it. The bottom of the displacer cylinder is kept hot (by boiling water, for example), while the top stays cold. As the displacer piston moves up, the air inside is moved from the cold end to the hot end, where it expands.

Because the displacer is connected to the working piston, the expanding air goes up the tube, and pushes the piston. But the displacer is also connected to the flywheel; as the flywheel turns it moves the displacer down, the air is pushed back to the cold end, contracts, and pulls the piston back again. Then the cycle repeats itself.

Why is the Stirling engine so good? For one thing, it's very convenient: you can use any type of fuel, as long as it gets the hot part of the engine up to temperature. So a little model Stirling engine can run on a cup of tea, or even on a plate of haggis. And apart from being convenient, because you burn fuel on the outside of the engine you can arrange to burn it in the most efficient way. This you can't do in an internal combustion engine – which is why they spew out carbon monoxide and other pollutants.

In the second and third patents, Robert is named jointly with his brother James, an engineer. It looks as if Robert had the original vision, but James certainly helped to get the engines made in the foundries in which he worked.

One Stirling engine was lost for many years, and then dug out of a barn by the man who later became Lord Kelvin, Professor of Natural Philosophy at the University of Glasgow. He used it as the subject of his first talk to the Glasgow Philosophical Society. So trying to explain

how the Stirling engine worked was the beginning of Kelvin's work on heat, which culminated in his absolute scale of temperature and the laws of thermo-dynamics.

However, the Stirling engine didn't catch on. It was used for a while to power church organs, because it was so quiet and easy to use. Today it is used in rather specialist applications, including cryo-genics, because if you drive a Stirling engine with another engine, it actually pumps heat out of its surroundings.

Why did it never become popular? Clearly, it was way ahead of its time. People didn't really understand how it worked – some people suggested that it was true perpetual motion, which scientists scoffed at. Fuel economy is a popular idea now, but then coal was cheap. The materials available weren't really up to the job either. If they had been invented in the age of steel, Stirling engines would have been much more impressive. Finally, Robert and James Stirling didn't really exploit the ideas, either, and certainly didn't contest patents which infringed their own.

But what is amazing is that a minister, without any connection to the world of industry, should have the vision to see that a new sort of engine was possible, and the skill to make it work, and that he should have done it before most people had even seen a steam train. And it wasn't until 1878, the year Stirling *died*, that Karl Benz patented the first internal combustion engine.

There aren't many traces of Robert Stirling, but his engines flourish; try The Stirling Society, 7 Flint Hill, Dorking, Surrey RH4 2LL (01372 360363); engines are sold by Sterling Stirling, 15 The Pill, Newport, Gwent NP6 4JH; or try this excellent website: http://www.mech.saitama-u.-ac.jp/kiriki/links/.

BUILDING BLOCKS AND ROADS

Rushing about in our modern world, we often overlook some basic building blocks, such as the roads we use and the cement that holds our houses together. Roads and cement have not always been there; someone had to find out how to make them, and those pioneering civil engineers were in many ways just as heroic as the inventors of steam engines and weather forecasts; indeed much of their work has survived for centuries.

41. JOHN METCALFE – 'BLIND JACK' OF KNARESBOROUGH

John Metcalfe, better known as 'Blind Jack', is buried in the pretty graveyard at Spofforth, near Wetherby in North Yorkshire. The gravestone carries a terrific heroic tribute, which begins:

Here lies John Metcalfe
One whose infant sight
Felt the dark pressure of an endless night
Yet such the fervour of his dauntless mind
His limbs full sprung, his spirit unconfined
That long ere yet life's bolder years began
His sightless efforts marked the aspiring man.

It seems a bit over the top, but if ever a pioneer deserved to be called a hero, Blind Jack was that man. His ingenuity was matched by his personal bravery. Metcalfe was born in Knaresborough in 1717. When he was just six he caught smallpox

Blind Jack's grave in Spofforth, North Yorkshire.

and went completely blind. But he didn't let this stop him doing what all small boys do – climbing trees, leading apple-raiding expeditions in local orchards, learning to swim and even to dive. On one occasion at the High Bridge over the River Nidd in Knaresborough two men fell into the river. They sent for Blind Jack who dived again and again into the black water. One man was swept away, but on Jack's fourth dive he brought the other to the surface – sadly too late, as he had already drowned.

But Blind Jack was inventive as well as courageous and he became the first scientific builder of roads. In the 1750s the roads were scandalously bad. Although it is only 20 miles from Leeds to York, the journey by stagecoach could take eight hours; to get there for lunch you had to leave at four o'clock in the morning! On one occasion, Jack was in London and met his patron Colonel Lidell. The colonel kindly offered Jack a ride back to Harrogate in his coach, but Jack declined, claiming he couldn't afford the time. So they both set off for Yorkshire, the colonel in his coach and Jack on foot. Being completely blind, and having never walked the route before, Jack got seriously lost twice. It took him six days to walk home; the colonel in his coach took eight. So in 1765 Blind Jack decided there might be a future in building really good roads.

Clearly the difficult roads were the ones through boggy ground, and these were the ones Blind Jack tackled. Previously, road-makers either had to build roads around the bogs or, if that wasn't possible, they would dig the bog out. Unfortunately, this meant that the new road was lower than the surrounding wet ground and it acted as a drain. Jack invented a new system of floating the roads on rafts. First, he would dig trenches on either side of the proposed route, heaping the material dug out into the middle where it would dry out. He then collected heather for his raft, layering the twigs of heather first down the length of the road, then across. Finally he would put the stone roadway on top. Jack's attempt to build a road from Huddersfield to Saddleworth across the top of the Pennines became a public event. He employed up to 400 people, and crowds gathered to watch, confident that when the road opened the horses would sink into the mire. Instead they sailed across, and that stretch was the driest part of the road, working without repair for twelve years.

Although the roads themselves have now been overgrown, you can follow the routes Blind Jack laid over the Pennines, and at Devil's Clough near Marsden one of his wonderful dry-stone bridges survives. Jack's involvement in the roads was total: even though he couldn't see where he was going he surveyed the routes himself, a solitary figure 6 foot 2 inches tall and equipped with just a measuring wheel and stick. Yet he was able to describe in remarkable detail the routes he had planned, and the types of soil the road would pass over. In all he made 180 miles of road, earning £65,000.

Blind Jack led a pretty exciting life – eloping with a publican's daughter on the eve of her wedding, acting as recruiting officer on the king's side during the 1745 rebellion, smuggling, and earning money as a wonderful roving fiddle-player. Almost beyond belief were his horse-riding skills which he matched with his knack as a gambler to make quite a lot of money. He once bet that he could ride an unbroken horse at full gallop for 200 yards, and then bring it to a complete stop within 50. Naturally punters happily bet against this

Blind Jack, out surveying roads.

unlikely boast but Blind Jack had a brilliant plan. He took the horse to a bog, paced out 200 yards, pointed the horse towards the bog and let it loose. As he had promised it galloped for 200 yards and then came to an immediate stop in the bog, whence it had to be hauled out by rope.

There was an annual race in Knaresborough forest which involved riding round a circular 3-mile course marked by posts – not the most obvious challenge for a blind man. Again heavily bet against, Jack persuaded friends to stand by each post with a dinner bell. Jack was able to win the race by riding towards the sound of each bell in turn. Despite his spectacularly dangerous hobbies, Jack lived to be ninety-three, and left behind ninety great-grandchildren.

You will find Blind Jack's gravestone in Spofforth churchyard.

42. ELEANOR COADE AND HER STONE: BUCKINGHAM PALACE AND RIO ZOO

Eleanor Coade invented, and for fifty years produced, the first successful artificial stone: a ceramic material so durable that 650 pieces survive to this day, in fireplaces, statues, ornaments and doorways. She made stone for George III and George IV, and received commissions from all over Britain, from North and South America, the Caribbean, Poland and Russia.

The Coade family came originally from Coad's Green in Cornwall. Eleanor (christened Elinor) was born in Exeter on 24 June 1733, where her father George was a prosperous wool finisher. Unfortunately, the wool business declined, and he went bankrupt first in 1759, and then again in 1769. The second time his house and belongings were sold, and he died soon afterwards.

Luckily Eleanor had already moved to London and established herself in business. In that same year, 1769, she set up in Narrow Wall, Lambeth (now Belvedere Road) as a maker of artificial stone. Her mother joined her there, and there has been much confusion because she also was called Eleanor. Furthermore, the daughter called herself Mrs Coade for respectability in business. In fact she never married, partly perhaps because she was an ardent feminist and was reluctant to allow her husband to acquire all her possessions and her business, as he would have done until the Married Women's Property Act of 1882. In her will she left money to several widows and spinsters, and to some married women, on condition that their husbands could not touch it, and that contrary to normal practice, they signed for the legacies themselves 'notwithstanding their coverture!' She also left £100 to the Girls' Charity School at Walworth, but only £50 to the Boys'.

Her factory flourished from the beginning in 1769 until she died in 1821, and indeed carried on into the 1830s in the hands of the man who had been her manager. Several patents had been taken out for artificial stone before she came on the scene, but none of the processes really worked. We do not know how she found a winner, but she certainly did, and her product was ceramic – a type of pottery.

There are three kinds of pottery: earthenware, which is weak and porous and used for flowerpots; stoneware, which is stronger and used for casseroles; and porcelain, which is very strong but impossible to work in large quantities, because the stuff is almost liquid before firing. Eleanor made stoneware; she used ball clay from Devon and Cornwall, mixed it with 10 per cent grog (crushed stoneware), 5–10 per cent of flint, and 5–10 per cent of fine sand. The mixture was rolled out like pastry, pressed into moulds, finished or fettled, and finally fired at 1100–1150°C. Pressing the cold wet clay mix into the moulds was tedious, fiddly work, and she probably used children to do it: some very small fingerprints have been found in the stone!

Robert Adam had come back from Italy in 1758 bursting with enthusiasm for neo-classical architecture, so elegant stonework was popular. He used loads of Coade stone, and many others followed. Her stone was used for fancy doorways, for statues, for urns and other stone ornaments, and for commemorative pediments; its one great advantage was that unlike real stone, Coade stone did not erode – it was impervious to weathering.

A Scale of two Feet.

The River God, Eleanor Coade's greatest work in Lythodipyra or Coade stone, was fired in one piece at her Lambeth factory. It is now at Ham House in Surrey.

Among surviving examples of Coade stone some can still be found in Buckingham Palace, St George's Chapel, Windsor, the Royal Naval College at Greenwich, and even the entrance to the zoo in Rio de Janeiro. The best-known pieces are the huge lion on the southern end of Westminster Bridge and the tomb of Captain Bligh. There is a wonderful river god at Ham House in Surrey, and an impressive doorway at Schomberg House, half way up Pall Mall.

Eleanor's uncle Sam had lived in Lyme Regis, and in 1784 he gave her his house, which was then called Bunter's Castle, and is now called Belmont; it is still dressed with her stone. The secret formula of her stone was finally worked out by analysis of a fragment from the top of one of the gateposts.

Very few women managed to establish successful businesses in the eighteenth century; she must have had three exceptional talents: for discovering such a successful formula for what she called 'Lithodipyra' and making it work; for either being or employing a fine artist and making attractive statues which appealed to the public; and for being a brilliant businesswoman and entrepreneur.

The easiest pieces of Coade stone to see are the lion on the south end of Westminster Bridge and the doorway of Schomberg House, half way up the south side of Pall Mall. But Alison Kelly's book lists hundreds of others. Eleanor used a horse-mill for grinding the stone. This was discovered in 1950, and the bed of the mill – the bottom stone – is now set into the paving by the river bank in front of the Royal Festival Hall, although there is no plaque. The best news is that Mrs Coade's secret formula didn't die with her; in Dorset, Philip Thomason has analysed her stone, worked out the recipe and is now making Coade stone again.

43. JOSEPH ASPDIN AND HIS PORTLAND CEMENT

Portland cement is one of the most important raw materials in the building trade. Hardly a building goes up in the industrialised countries of the world without its share of Portland cement, and sometimes vast structures are made entirely of cement, with merely some sand and gravel aggregate to turn it into concrete, and some reinforcing rods to add tensile strength. By one of those delightful quirks of fate, Portland cement was invented as the result of a careless mistake by a bricklayer in Leeds.

Concrete has a long history: it was used for the floors of huts on the banks of the Danube in about 5600 BC; in the construction of the Great Pyramid of Giza

Primitive cement has been around for five thousand years — Hadrian's Wall is held together with 'Roman' cement.

in 2500 BC; and spectacularly by the Romans. They found they could make strong cements by using volcanic ash from Vesuvius. The dome of the Pantheon in Rome is almost 50 yards across, and is made of a lightweight concrete using pumice stone as aggregate; this dome inspired Christopher Wren when he came to design St Paul's Cathedral. Similarly, the Pont du Gard aqueduct and Hadrian's Wall were held together with concrete.

John Smeaton, commissioned in 1756 to build the third Eddystone lighthouse, experimented with types of concrete that would set under water, and eventually produced a complex mixture of burnt Aberthaw blue lias (Welsh limestone) and Italian pozzolana, which was the best cement produced since the Romans left – and Smeaton's Stump still stands on the Eddystone rocks to prove it! Because Portland stone had an excellent reputation as a building material, Smeaton set out to make a cement that would not only look as good but also be as strong as Portland stone, and he called it Portland cement. But the most important advance in technology came seventy years later, in a grubby back yard in Yorkshire.

On Christmas Day 1778, Thomas Aspdin, a bricklayer of Hunslet near Leeds, celebrated when his wife produced a son, whom they called Joseph. He followed in his father's footsteps and became a bricklayer, too. In 1817 he decided to cut out one of the middlemen and make his own cement, so he moved into Leeds and bought an old glassworks in Slip-in Yard, Back of Shambles, off Briggate. This was where his chemistry went wrong.

Simple lime mortars are made from chalk, limestone or shells, which are all forms of calcium carbonate ($CaCO_3$). Heating this in an oven at about 1000°C drives off carbon dioxide to produce quicklime (CaO). Adding water to quicklime makes slaked lime ($Ca(OH)_2$), which will mix with more water to make a smooth paste of lime mortar. This mortar is easy to work with, and it sticks bricks together slowly but effectively, because although it does not set on its own, it reacts very slowly with the carbon dioxide in the atmosphere to make calcium carbonate, which is hard. Adding a little clay to the lime makes the cement harder, and it sets more strongly, although too much clay makes the mortar difficult to use.

Apparently Joseph Aspdin used a mixture of one part of clay to three parts of limestone, and he melted them together. Had he been using a lime kiln at around 1000°C that would have been fine, and he would have made conventional lime mortar. But his glass furnace was designed to reach higher temperatures, and probably by mistake he heated his mixture to about 1300°C. When he cooled it down again he found the furnace was full of lumps of clinker, so hard they were difficult to get out of the furnace. When he did get them out he had tremendous trouble grinding them into powder and his investment in the furnace must have seemed rather dubious. And when he found that the powder would not even slake properly, as lime should when mixed with water, he must have come close to abandoning the whole enterprise.

But then he discovered that this new powder behaved strangely with water.

The Ship-on-Shore pub, Sheerness. Hoping perhaps for something alcoholic, locals salvaged barrels from a shipwreck, only to find they were filled with cement — which set solid in the water. They put them to good use by building a pub.

Joseph Aspdin's first cement works in Wakefield.

Instead of just getting wet it reacted slowly to make a solid and insoluble mass: an incredibly strong artificial stone. Here at last was the product that everyone wanted – a cement that would set hard throughout its bulk, not merely on the surface. It would even set like a rock under water; John Smeaton would have been delighted. And when Aspdin applied for his patent in 1824, he followed Smeaton's example and called his new product Portland cement. He outgrew his little factory in Leeds, moved to larger premises in Wakefield, and made both cement and money.

The high temperature in the furnace was critical, for it causes the chalk and the clay to react together to produce a new compound: calcium silicate. This is the rock-like mass on which most of the world's buildings now stand. In fact, Joe Aspdin never really understood the potential of his creation. He thought of it merely as a material for facing brick buildings, to make them look like stone. He died on 20 March 1855, and was buried at St John's Chapel in Wakefield. He would have been amazed at a typical modern cement works, using huge rotating kilns to melt together a 3:1 mixture of chalk and clay at 1450°C, and producing 3,000 tonnes of Portland cement every day. And all because the brickie from Hunslet had bought a second-hand glassworks. . .

There remains one building still faced with Aspdin's original artificial stone – the Wakefield Arms pub, beside Kirkgate station in Wakefield. The smooth facing of the pub is a testimony to the quality of his product, and the lunch in the pub isn't bad either! A curious memorial is the Ship-on-Shore pub at Sheerness, which is made entirely from solidified barrels of cement. These were being transported down the Thames when the ship ran aground; local people thought the barrels contained whisky and quickly hauled them ashore, only to find they were full of rapidly hardening cement, so they turned the barrels into a pub!

44. THOMAS TELFORD, THE 'COLOSSUS OF ROADS', AND JOHN LOUDON MCADAM, WHO DID NOT THINK OF TAR

Thomas Telford was born in Dumfriesshire on 9 August 1757. He was apprenticed to a stonemason, and went to work with architects in London; by the 1790s he was heavily into canals, and then he moved on to roads. He became the greatest road-builder of his time. Telford surveyed and built many hundreds of miles of roads – about 900 miles in the Highlands of Scotland, where there had been almost none before he came, and 200 miles in the Lowlands – and the important road from London to Holyhead, which was the principal route to Ireland.

Telford said the road to Holyhead took him fifteen years of incessant labour, but what a wonderful job he made of it! Built in the early 1800s for horse-drawn coaches weighing perhaps a ton, it's still the main road 180 years later – the A5, carrying 30 ton juggernauts to the Irish ferries. To appreciate his wonderful skill, go to Snowdonia, to the lovely little town of Betws-y-Coed, where vigorous streams tumble down the hillside beside the road, and look at the Waterloo Bridge over the river. Built in 1815, it commemorates the great victory of the battle of Waterloo in cast-iron text under the arch.

Telford's road then heads north-west from Betws-y-Coed past Lake Ogwen and over the Nant Ffrancon pass to Bangor. The country is dramatic, and the hills are high, but Thomas Telford surveyed and planned this road so skilfully that the gradient is never as steep as 1 in 20 – which is really easy on a mountain bike – although I'd be a bit happier without the howling wind that usually seems to blow. Mind you, the day we went there to film, the wind was so strong it blew me up the hill at about 15 mph without my having to pedal!

This road through Snowdonia is evidence of Telford's skill as a surveyor, and he also developed strict rules about how to do the actual construction. He suggested in later years that the way to become an

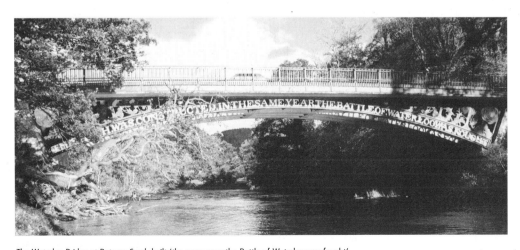

The Waterloo Bridge at Betws-y-Coed, built 'the same year the Battle of Waterloo was fought'.

engineer was to start by working as a labourer, and get your hands dirty. 'This', he said, 'is the true way of acquiring practical skill, a thorough knowledge of the materials employed in construction, and at last but not least, a perfect knowledge of the habits and disposition of the workmen who carry out our designs.'

On some of his inspection trips he took along his friend, the poet Robert Southey, who described his methods:

First, level and drain, then, like the Romans, lay a solid pavement of large stones, the round or broad end downwards, as close as they can be set; the points are then broken off, and a layer of stones about the size of walnuts laid over them;. . . over all a little gravel if it be at hand. . .

Telford himself specified that the road should always be 20 feet wide, including a strip of turf at each side. The roadway should be 14 inches deep in the middle, and 9 inches at the sides – so there was a good camber to encourage the rain to run off. The material should be 'gravel of a proper quality, out of which all stones above the size of a hen's egg shall have been previously taken' – although it was all right to use bigger stones at the bottom. The iron tyres of stage coaches crushed the grit into the gaps between the stones and made a smooth surface that rain could not easily penetrate.

Telford also built more than a thousand bridges, and one of the most impressive was to get across the Menai Straits to Anglesey, 200 yards across vicious tides and deep water. The Admiralty insisted that the bridge must be high enough to let the largest ships sail below with masts erect, and he couldn't make a timber frame to build an arch over the top, because they would not allow even a temporary obstruction. Telford designed an amazing suspension bridge, easily the longest in the world at the time. At each end he planned a massive tower, 153 feet above the high water mark. Between them he would hang sixteen chains, and then the roadway would be built hanging from the chains, 579 feet long and 30 feet wide.

The chains were made of 9 foot links, each of thirty-six iron bars half an inch square. Would it be possible to lift these massive chains up the towers? For several nights, as tension mounted, the normally imperturbable Telford was unable to sleep. Finally, on 26 April 1825, hundreds of people on the banks and on boats watched as the chain was floated underneath on a massive raft, and then winched up on cables by 150 men heaving on capstans. When it reached the top of the tower there was a colossal cheer, and three men walked high above the sea to the other tower across the 9 inch wide chain!

On 30 January 1826 the Menai Bridge was opened for traffic, and at 1.35 a.m. the Down Royal London and Holyhead mail coach rumbled over the bridge through blackest night and howling wind. In the morning everyone wanted to cross: flags flew, bands played, and cannons crashed as coach after coach struggled through the heavy rain; so many, in fact, that there was actually a traffic jam on the bridge. Before the bridge was built, 13,000 travellers a year used to cross the Straits by ferry. The crossing took 45 minutes in good weather. The ferry yielded an income of over £800 a year to

Telford's Menai Bridge, connecting Anglesey with the rest of Wales.

Miss Williams of Plas Isa, who, when the bridge was built, was granted compensation of £26,557!

A few miles to the east, Telford also built the Conwy Bridge, 327 feet long and designed to match the castle; here, he used a rope sling. The bridge was opened on 1 July 1826 just after noon and first across was the Chester Mail with as many passengers as could possibly find a place on board. The route was solid with spectators, singing 'God Save the King' as loud as they could. There was much revelry; windows were broken in the pubs. Thomas Telford was sixty-nine.

Telford did almost all his greatest work before the coming of trains, but he built many miles of canals. He built the Caledonian Canal, linking the Atlantic with the North Sea via Loch Ness and the Great Glen, with twenty-nine locks. He built the even longer Gotha Canal across Sweden: 53 miles of new canal in a total

navigation stretching 238 miles from sea to sea. When he first went to Sweden with two assistants in July 1808 it was his first trip abroad, and he was clearly a bit worried about vital rations, because for the six-day voyage he took extensive supplies, including three 40-lb hams, 90 lb of biscuits and 33 lb of lump sugar, not to mention forty-eight bottles of wine, six bottles of gin and six bottles of brandy. It must have been a jolly trip!

But one of the most beautiful and elegant of all his canal works was also one of the earliest: Pont Cysyllte, which was completed in 1805. This carries the Ellesmere Canal 127 feet above the River Dee in north-east Wales. All previous aqueducts had been massive chunky affairs just a few feet above the river, but Telford introduced a brand new idea – his 'stream in the sky' runs in a cast-iron trough 11 feet 10 inches wide and 1007 feet long; the trough sits on a bridge of eighteen tapering stone piers, 20×12 feet at river level and 13×7 feet 6 inches at the top. The Pont Cysyllte aqueduct was opened on 26 November 1805; six boats sailed majestically across, and there was much rejoicing. This amazing construction was probably what made Thomas Telford famous, and it stands firm and unchanged, 191 years later, as a monument to his genius. Sir Walter Scott called it the greatest work of art he had ever seen.

Telford's life was full of extraordinary events. In 1788, early in his career, the churchwardens asked him to look at St Chad's Church in Shrewsbury, because the roof was leaking. At the next meeting he told them they needn't worry about the roof until they had taken urgent action to secure the walls. They laughed at him, and said the cracks had been there for hundreds of years – was he looking for work or something? So he walked out, suggesting they should continue their meeting outside in the churchyard. Three days later the church clock struck, and the entire tower collapsed through the roof of the nave. . . .

Hero memorials come in many shapes and sizes, from shopping centres to British Telecom offices, but there aren't many heroes who have had entire towns named after them. In Telford Civic Square in Telford New Town stands a fine bronze statue of the man whom the poet Robert Southey called 'the colossus of roads'.

The same label was later attached to another contemporary road-builder, John Loudon McAdam. McAdam was born on 21 September 1756 into a fairly well-off Scottish family in Ayrshire, and in due course was sent to the colony of New York to be apprenticed to an uncle as a merchant. He was successful, and made a lot of money, but after the War of Independence he returned to Scotland, bought an estate near Ayr, and began looking after the roads there. He also bought into the British Tar Company, but it turned out to be a disaster, and he had to sell his estate to pay off his debts.

In 1798 he was appointed agent for revictualling the navy in the western ports, and moved to Falmouth, but he remained interested in roads, and claimed that during the next ten years he travelled 30,000 miles around Britain, inspecting the roads, at his own expense. In 1815 he was appointed general surveyor of the roads belonging to the Bristol Turnpike Trust. This put him in charge of 178 miles of roads, and paid him a salary of £400 a year.

The turnpike trusts were supposed to maintain the roads. They had been conceived as money-spinning ventures for local landowners, but in fact were hopeless, inefficient, and a financial drain. By 1812 the Bristol Turnpike Trust had debts of £44,000.

The trusts were under some pressure from the postmaster-general, since the superintendent of mail-coaches reckoned the roads constituted 'a very considerable evil'. If they received enough complaints about a stretch of road, the trustees would get a farmer to hire some labourers, send them to a quarry for stones and dump them on the road. As a result of this type of treatment, the roads gradually became impassable. Big stones caused the worst problems: either they were simply pushed aside by the cartwheels, or they forced wheels to climb over them. This often caused damage to the wheel or to the road when the wheel came down again – and some carriages were liable to turn over.

McAdam realised the most important thing was to use small stones, and he devised simple procedures for making and measuring them. He said large stones should be broken by men, but the small stones should be made by women or old men, while sitting down (those 'past hard labour' could sit on straw mats); thus he employed whole families, which was highly popular. He specified that the women and old men should use hammers no more than 15 inches long with a one-inch face, to produce stones less than an inch across: 'Every stone which is put into a road which exceeds an inch in any of its dimensions is mischievous.' He apparently told workers on site that any stone too big to fit inside their mouths was too big to go on the road.

Using small stones and compressing them to make a firm surface that was smooth for wheels and resisted rain, McAdam rapidly made the roads passable more cheaply than before. He expanded his operation by offering to survey for free the roads of other turnpike trusts, and then offering to repair them at a discount. Then he passed on the work to his sons, nephews or sons-in-law. The family became rich again, and controlled great lengths of road.

He published two accounts of his methods: *A practical essay on the scientific repair and preservation of roads* (1819) and *Present state of road-making* (1820), which went through several editions. In 1827 Parliament made him general surveyor of roads, gave him £10,000, and offered him a knighthood, which he refused. He died in 1836.

His methods were undoubtedly successful, and the word macadamise entered the English language: 'to make or repair a road according to J.L. McAdam's system, which consists in laying down successive layers of stone broken into pieces of nearly uniform size, each layer being allowed to consolidate under the pressure of ordinary wheel traffic before the next is laid upon it' (OED). He further specified that there should be no sort of foundation beneath the stones, and that no gravel, sand or earth should be used as binding agent.

He said it was quite wrong to dig a trench first – rather the road should be raised above the surrounding ground – and he did not care what he built on, even soft earth was fine. Indeed he did experiments to show that a road built on a soft base lasted longer than one built on rock. McAdam said that the total thickness of stone should be about 10 inches, and explained that under pressure of the traffic the sharp angles of the stones united into a compact mass, entirely impervious to moisture. He said the standard road 18 feet wide should be 3 inches higher in the middle than at the edges, so that the rain would run off, and he expected the building of such a road to cost a shilling a running yard, or £88 per mile.

What is perhaps ironic is that tarmac had nothing to do with him: the idea of using tar on roads apparently did not occur to McAdam, even though he had been involved in the tar business. Tarmac came about after an accidental tar spillage in Yorkshire, many years after the death of John Loudon McAdam.

Thomas Telford's monuments are many. His statue in Telford is perhaps the most obvious, but my favourites are the bridges at Menai, Conwy, and Betws-y-Coed, and the fabulous 'stream in the sky' at Pont Cysyllte, near Llangollen. Traces of McAdam are harder to find, but there is a plaque on his house in Berkeley Square in Bristol.

45. JOSEPH PAXTON AND THE CRYSTAL PALACE

Although it sounds unlikely, giant lily leaves brought together the two best-known activities of Joseph Paxton, the extraordinary man who not only transformed the grounds at Chatsworth in Derbyshire, but also built the Crystal Palace for the Great Exhibition of 1851. Joseph Paxton was born in Bedfordshire on 3 August 1801, the son of a poor tenant farmer who died soon afterwards. When he left school, Joseph was sent to work on his brother's farm, where he was beaten and starved, but not paid. When he was seventeen he ran away to be a gardener.

He was determined to better himself, and always made the most of every position he got into. He had a succession of gardening jobs, and at Chiswick Gardens Arboretum became foreman, but because he earned only eighteen shillings a week, he had just decided to go to America to earn more, when one day he opened the door for the Duke of Devonshire, who owned Chiswick Gardens and lived next door. The duke took an instant liking to the lad, and although he was only twenty-three appointed him superintendent at his country home – Chatsworth House in Derbyshire. Wow! What a break!

On his first day at Chatsworth, Paxton was understandably nervous and keyed up. He arrived at 4.30 a.m., explored the grounds, climbed over the wall into the walled garden, set the men to work, watched the water-works in action, joined the housekeeper Mrs Gregory for breakfast, met her niece Sarah Brown and

fell instantly in love – they eventually married and had a daughter – and all this before nine o'clock in the morning!

The Duke of Devonshire thought Paxton was wonderful, and more or less gave him a free hand with the gardens, so he set about building all sorts of magnificent display pieces. He made huge fountains, one of which spouts water up to 270 feet – twice the height of Nelson's Column. There is also a magnificent cascade of water down what is essentially a long flight of stone steps. The water for these displays came from a lake at the top of the hill behind the house. There are no pumps: gravity does all the work, and the high fountain can still be switched on just by turning a tap.

Paxton built an arboretum, a conservatory 300 feet long, and even a model village – Edensor. Apparently the duke was impressed by an architectural catalogue, and simply ordered one of each model! So every house is different. The duke adopted Paxton as a companion and confidant; they went everywhere together, and took one long trip around the Mediterranean.

In 1837 a traveller brought back from Guyana a fantastic new lily, but the experts at Kew Gardens were unable to get it to grow. Paxton got hold of a cutting, and designed a specially heated pool, using water-wheels to keep the water flowing. He managed to make the lily grow, and even he was staggered by its size. In three months it had eleven 5 foot leaves, and huge flowers. He named it *Victoria regia*, and gave Queen Victoria a bud. This lily was far too big to grow in most conservatories, and Paxton had to work out a way of

Joseph Paxton, builder of the Crystal Palace.

designing bigger spaces. He wanted glass overhead, and he needed to dream up some simple structure that would hold up the glass. Inspired by the huge leaves of the lily, which were themselves a feat of engineering, he said, he tried floating his daughter Annie on a leaf and it worked.

So he designed a rigid structure made of radiating ribs connected by flexible cross-ribs. He tried it out, modified it, tried Mark 2, modified it again, and so on, until he got it to work. He used wood, because it was cheap and light, and he made the glass roof in ridges and furrows so that the maximum amount of light came in – even during the early morning and late evening light wasn't wasted by reflection. He designed special rafters that had gutters above the glass to collect rainwater and below the glass to collect condensation. For support he used hollow pillars that doubled as drainpipes. But the really brilliant idea behind the final design was that all the pieces were prefabricated, and simply bolted together on site. He designed the machines to make the parts, which were then manufactured in vast numbers.

In 1851 there was to be a Great Exhibition in Hyde Park in London. Clearly they needed a temporary building to house it, and a competition was held for the design of this structure. The judges included the great railway engineers George Stephenson and Isambard Kingdom Brunel, who rejected all 245 entries, and suggested their own plan, but this was so ugly it was turned down after a public outcry.

Joseph Paxton offered to put in a design, and was given two weeks. Within nine days he had on their desks a stunning version of his lily-leaf-supported greenhouse. It was simple to erect, it could easily be taken down again after the exhibition, and it was amazingly cheap – only £80,000 for a building big enough to hold twelve football pitches on the ground floor, and more than 100 feet high. Paxton raised the stakes by publishing his design in the *Illustrated London News*.

The building – the 'Millennium Dome' of 1851 – attracted great interest and disapproval in the press, and the magazine *Punch* sneeringly called it the Crystal Palace. Some authorities feared it would attract thieves and prostitutes, but the people loved it. In fact the whole thing was a phenomenal success, and

The Crystal Palace, built in Hyde Park to house the Great Exhibition of 1851.

Paxton was knighted, and became Sir Joseph Paxton.

There was a bit of a problem before it opened, because it was built with two huge elm trees inside, and a mass of sparrows came in out of the cold and nested in the elms, and made a lot of mess. How on earth could they get rid of the sparrows? Shooting was obviously impossible, with all that glass. The queen summoned the Duke of Wellington, and he, resourceful as ever, said, 'Well ma'am, you could try a sparrowhawk'. Biological control, in 1851!

The public lavatories in the Crystal Palace were installed by flamboyant plumber George Jennings, who decided to charge people a penny to go in. There was a storm of protest, but 827,280 visitors did indeed 'spend a penny' – which is probably where that expression came from! After the Great Exhibition, the Crystal Palace was taken down, piece by piece, and re-erected at Sydenham, where Paxton went to live. He became rich, famous, and Member of Parliament for Coventry, and died in 1865. The Crystal Palace was destroyed by a fire in 1936.

Chatsworth is open to the public, and has magnificent grounds, which still owe much to Paxton's inventiveness; in particular the great fountain and the water cascade are strikingly attractive, and there is a camellia planted in 1851 and therefore perhaps by him, in one of his original arboretums. There's also an excellent and reasonably priced lunch to be had in the restaurant.

46. DONALD BAILEY AND HIS BRIDGE TO VICTORY

Sir Donald Coleman Bailey's invention was hardly glamorous. Indeed it was so simple and unassuming that at first it was ignored in favour of more complicated designs. But in the end, his revolutionary bridge proved to be a vital link in the road to victory in Europe in 1944 and 1945.

Bailey came from Rotherham, went to Sheffield University and got his first job with Rowntree in York, before joining the Military Engineering Experimental Establishment in 1928 as a civil engineering designer. The problem he was to solve so spectacularly well was familiar from many military campaigns. In retreat, as the Allies had been, you cut communications and blow bridges to hold up the progress of the enemy. But what happens when the tables are turned and you need to invade? The tactics that had been so sensible in retreat make an attack almost impossible. In the Second World War the problem was worse than in any preceding conflict because aerial bombing had been able to destroy an amazingly high proportion of bridges. Bailey had in fact dreamed up the design for a bridge as early as 1936, but the War Office wasn't interested. Bailey must have been sure his design was right, because he kept working at it in his own time.

By 1941 the government had realised that a portable military bridge would indeed be necessary in Europe, and settled on a design by Charles Inglis. Bailey had seen the design and predicted that it wasn't strong enough – a prediction fulfilled when the Inglis Bridge failed under test. This could have set the war back – but luckily Colonel Fowle had seen Bailey's design sketched on the back of an envelope (which seems too good to be true) and asked him to work it up. Bailey was ordered to go ahead in February 1941, but because he had been working on the design in private the first prototype was ready by 5 May. The idea was simple: the bridge was made up from a kit of components, the key one being the panel, 10 feet by 5 feet, made of steel girders, and reinforced in a diamond pattern. The panel was small enough to fit into a standard 3-ton army truck, strong enough to make a bridge that could carry a tank, but light enough to be carried by six soldiers. The panels were joined by beams that could also be carried by a few men, and the whole lot bolted together in a wonderfully low-tech way so that on the front line you didn't need specialists to do the work.

He doesn't look like a war hero, but Donald Bailey's bridge helped secure victory in the Second World War.

The brilliance of the Bailey Bridge lay in its simplicity and versatility. With little training, ordinary soldiers could bridge a ditch — or the Rhine.

Naturally the bridge had to be tested. The 70 foot span was completed in just thirty-six minutes, then loaded up with a 1917 Mark V tank filled with pig iron. It must have been a tense moment, remembering the fate of the Inglis Bridge, but the Bailey Bridge passed with flying colours and was soon in production. The first bridges went into service in December 1941, just ten months after Bailey was given the order to proceed, and entirely due to the faith its inventor had had in his own idea and the unpaid work he had done to develop it.

The bridges were a tremendous success. Between 1944 and 1945 two thousand Bailey Bridges were erected in north-west Europe alone, and one general reckoned the Bailey Bridge doubled the value of Allied armoured and mechanised units. The Bailey Bridge solved one of the trickiest problems in bridge-building. It was in the nature of the situations in which they were used that the bridges would often have to be built from one side of a river or chasm, with no hope of getting men on to the far bank. Bailey simply rolled the bridge from one bank to the other, the first part to cross being a lightweight 'nose' that would later be discarded, and always making sure that enough bridge had been built on land to counter-balance the part suspended in mid-air.

The system was so versatile that huge engineering projects could be undertaken with the panel and beam kit, and Bailey's name became legendary among Allied troops. He was rewarded with an OBE before the war ended, and a knighthood in 1946. The bridges lived on after the war, one being bought for £300 as surplus and erected over the River Don by Rotherham Corporation and the neighbouring Rawmarsh Urban Development Council as a tribute to Donald Bailey.

COMMUNICATIONS

Since even before the invention of speech, hominids have wanted to communicate. The first grunted instructions for how to hunt animals or make baskets gave way to elaborate story telling, singing and remembering with advantages. Steadily advancing technology made the storage and retrieval of information ever more efficient, through books, computers and the Internet, and now we have so many ways of communicating with one another, and we are so overwhelmed by junk mail and mobile phones, that we forget how difficult were the first steps in communication at a distance.

47. SAMUEL MORLAND'S MEGAPHONES

Samuel Morland was a member of the Secret Service. He was instrumental in restoring Charles II to the throne, and became his chief mechanic. Although he was vain and a bit of a fool, he pumped water higher than anyone had before, and conducted pioneering experiments in long-distance voice communication.

Samuel Morland, the son of a vicar, was probably born in Sulhampstead in Berkshire in 1625. At that time England was in political upheaval. By the time Samuel left Cambridge University, Parliament had thrown out the King, and Cromwell was running the country. Morland became a staunch supporter of the new government, and got himself sent to Sweden and France as a diplomat, doubtless because of his skills as a linguist.

Morland's character wasn't particularly attractive. He went to great lengths to keep in with people in authority, and was often regarded as a bit of a fool by those who witnessed his fawning. But he did have some very particular skills. He was the best man in Britain at opening, copying and resealing letters without detection; he claimed to have invented a method for quickly reproducing wax seals; and he could copy a page of writing in just a minute, probably by pressing a damp tissue paper over the surface of a letter. He could also forge handwriting. Not surprisingly, this led to a job in the Secret Service, privy to the secrets of state, a position which was to entirely change his beliefs – and his fortune.

One night in 1658 Morland was taking a nap at his desk when Cromwell came to see his boss, Thurloe. They discussed a plot to lure the exiled Charles II back to England – and then kill him. Cromwell suddenly noticed Morland, drew his sword and was about to run him through, but Thurloe said that he had been working through the previous two nights and was genuinely asleep. Morland was appalled by what he heard, and decided to switch support to the king, sending him money and details of the plot. Charles is supposed to have been pulling on his boots for the journey to England when the message arrived. In 1659 Morland went to Holland to see Charles, who knighted him. Sir Samuel made sure the king agreed to give him a huge pension as well.

Sir Samuel Morland, *Magister Mechanicorum* (Master of Mechanics).

Morland's talent for invention ensured his popularity with Charles II, our most scientific monarch, who went on to found the Royal Society, for many years the centre of British science. So it was to science rather than diplomacy that Morland turned in order to curry favour with the monarch, and his most famous invention, devised in 1670, went by the magnificent name of *tuba stentoro-phonica*.

The horn or trumpet was an ancient instrument, and had been used for ages to signal troops – Alexander the Great allegedly used one to give orders at a distance of 100 stadia (about 12 miles). But apparently Alexander's horn was a sort of musical instrument, played not unlike modern brass instruments, where the player makes a sort of refined 'raspberry' sound in the mouthpiece which the instrument amplifies. Morland wondered whether the trumpet could be modified for amplifying speech. He designed and made several trumpets of different shapes and materials, the first in glass in 1670.

It was about 32 inches long, 11 inches in diameter at the large end and 2½ inches at the small end. He then switched to more practical brass instruments, the next being much bigger at about 4½ feet long. This second instrument was the subject of two royal trials in St James's Park. In the first, the Lord Angier stood by the park wall near Goring House and heard Morland speaking from the end of the Mall near Old Spring Garden. In the second, the king, Prince Rupert and various dignitaries stood at one end of the Mall, and heard Morland speaking from the other – an impressive 850 yards.

Encouraged by his success, Morland began to think big. He took a 17 foot long copper instrument down to the river below London Bridge and, leaving it with a waterman, rowed down to near Deptford from where he heard the waterman clearly – a distance of 1½ miles. The fourth machine was the biggest he made, at an unwieldy 21 feet long. Both giant horns were heard from 'over against Faux-Hall, to the nearest part of Battersey over against Chelsey; And at another from Hide-Park-Gate to Chelsey-Colledge' – again 1½ miles. He judged that a conversation could be maintained at a distance of ¾ mile.

After this, the largest three were sent to Deal Castle to be tested. The Governor, Francis Digby, reported on 14 October 1671 that speech was heard at Walmer Castle, a mile away. The largest one was tried successfully between the shore and ships at anchor 2 to 3 miles out. Charles II ordered some *tuba stentoro-phonicas* for his ships, and they did create excitement at the time. Morland also made a hearing trumpet with an equally magnificent name – the *otacousticon* – but it is not clear how this would have differed from the speaking trumpet.

Although he invented many silly things, including a portable clockwork kitchen, his pumps were really good. He once sent a jet of water, coloured with red wine, over 60 feet above the top of Windsor Castle. One spectator called it 'the boldest and most extraordinary experiment that has ever been performed by water in any part of the world'. Charles II was so pleased with this that on 14 August 1681 he summoned Morland and presented him with a gold medal studded with

The author on the Thames with his own version of the Morland megaphone, attempting to signal to some very cold Sea Cadets on the far bank.

diamonds, fastened to a green ribbon and bearing the inscription *Magister Mechanicorum* – Master of Mechanics!

Morland was spectacularly unlucky in love. His first four wives all died young, and his fifth marriage was a disaster. The woman was Mary Ayliff, an heiress – or so he thought. In fact, she turned out to be the daughter of a coachman, with no money at all, and she made Morland miserable and broke. Writing to Samuel Pepys he said, 'a criminal bound and going to execution is not in greater agonies than has been my poor active soul since this befell me', and signed himself 'your most humble but poor distressed servant, S. Morland'. Five months later, despite an appeal, a divorce was granted and he was rid of her.

Morland was clearly an ingenious man,

but a bit of a fool. If he had persisted with any of his schemes he might have become a distinguished scientist. He is even recorded as devising a steam engine, having worked out that water turning to steam expands in volume two thousand times. This would have been the first working steam engine in Britain. Instead his reputation is summed up by the reception of one of his calculating machines at the Royal Society: Robert Hooke described it as 'very silly'. Indeed the memory of Morland might have sunk without trace had he not done one brave thing, and saved the king's life, and it is because of the gratitude of Charles II that we have heard of Samuel Morland, *Magister Mechanicorum.*

Morland's best memorial is the megaphone. Try making your own with rolled-up newspaper, and see at what distance it can be heard.

48. ALEXANDER BAIN AND THE FAX MACHINE

The telephone was invented in 1875 by a Scotsman in America, and the instrument has utterly changed our lives. The fax machine brought about another substantial change when it came into general use in about the 1970s. I was astonished to discover that the fax machine was actually patented thirty years before the telephone was invented, by an ingenious shepherd from the north of Scotland called Alexander Bain.

Alexander Bain and his twin sister Margaret were born in October 1810. Their dad was a crofter, and he had six sisters and six brothers. They grew up in a remote stone cottage at Leanmore, a few miles north of Wick. The vast expanse of peaty countryside has only occasional scattered cottages, and the Bain house, close to a small wood, became a sheep byre, and is now little more than an outline of low stone walls. In the winter Sandy walked a mile or two to school in Backlass; in the summer he worked as a shepherd.

He was bottom of his class in school, and was a poor shepherd too, because he

The stones of the Bain family home at Leanmore, near Wick, have been made into a circular sheep-pen. Some of the original floor is still in place.

was always dreaming. But he was fascinated by clocks, and actually made himself a model clock using heather for the spring and the cogwheels, so his sympathetic father got him apprenticed to a clockmaker in Wick.

In January 1830 he walked 21 miles through the snow from Wick to Thurso to hear a lecture on 'Light, heat, and the electric fluid'. The lecture changed his life, for he decided then and there that electricity was the stuff to work with. He began inventing electrical devices, including various types of automatic telegraph, an electric clock, an earth battery, insulation for electric cables and an electric fire alarm. He took out patents on all these, and also on inkstands, inkholders and a ship's log. The most amazing idea he had was for what he called the electro-chemical telegraph, which we would call a fax machine. However, before he had a chance to develop it, he ran into an unpleasant spot of trouble in London.

In 1840 Bain was desperate for money to develop his clocks and his fax machine; he talked about his financial problems to the editor of the *Mechanics Magazine*, who introduced him to the well-known and highly respected Professor Sir Charles Wheatstone. Bain took his models to demonstrate at Wheatstone's house.

Wheatstone watched Bain's gadgets with fascination, and then, when asked for his opinion, said 'Oh, I shouldn't bother to develop these things any further! There's no future in them.' Bain went away disconsolate, but three months later Wheatstone went to the Royal Society and before the leaders of the scientific establishment demonstrated an electric clock, claiming it was his own invention. Luckily, Bain had already applied for his patent.

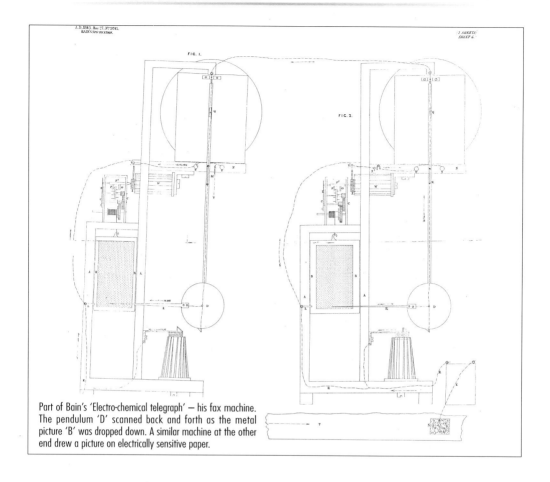

Part of Bain's 'Electro-chemical telegraph' — his fax machine. The pendulum 'D' scanned back and forth as the metal picture 'B' was dropped down. A similar machine at the other end drew a picture on electrically sensitive paper.

Professor Sir Charles Wheatstone had all the advantages of rank and social position, and did his level best to block Bain's patents. He failed, and rumours of his skulduggery began to circulate. So when Wheatstone organised an Act of Parliament to set up the Electric Telegraph Company, the House of Lords summoned Bain to give evidence, and eventually compelled the company to pay Bain £10,000 and give him a job as manager. Wheatstone resigned in a huff.

In 1841 Sandy Bain made a new kind of electric telegraph, the first of three devices he dreamed up to send pictures or printed words along telegraph wires. This was an idea decades ahead of its time: in

those days messages were sent by Morse code – people had to wait thirty years for the telephone – so even a skilled operator could send only a few words a minute. Bain's machine was to change all that.

Bain had already worked out how to set up a system of clocks that would remain exactly synchronised. He put a master clock in the railway station in Edinburgh, and another clock in the railway station in Glasgow. Then he arranged that every time the Edinburgh pendulum swung it sent a pulse of electricity along the telegraph wires, which drove a solenoid in Glasgow and pushed the Glasgow pendulum at exactly the same time. Bain's electrical mechanism didn't just make the clocks run at the same rate, it forced the pendulums to stay precisely in step.

When he wanted to send a picture along the wires, he made a copy of it in copper, and etched away everything but the lines he wanted. Then he arranged for a metal needle or stylus to swing across the picture. Each time it touched copper it made contact and sent a pulse along the telegraph wire.

The needle was attached to the pendulum of the clock at each end, so the positions of the contacts were faithfully reproduced at the receiving end by a matching stylus running across electro-sensitive paper; whenever there was a blip of current the stylus left a black mark on the paper, corresponding to the position of the line in the original picture.

Finally he arranged for both pictures – the one being sent and the one being received – to drop down by a millimetre at every swing of the pendulum. Thus the outgoing picture was gradually scanned by the stylus swinging across it and moving down line by line, and at the receiving end the new copy picture was gradually built up.

The whole concept was an outstanding example of pushing the available technology to its limits. Unfortunately, Bain, despite his ingenuity, was hopeless with money. He wasted lots in litigation in America, and lots more on trying to achieve perpetual motion. He eventually died in Glasgow, poor and sad, in 1877.

Wheatstone is famous, Bain is forgotten. But the man who invented the fax machine, a vital feature of every office today, was that unknown shepherd from Caithness, Alexander Bain.

The main Telecom building in Thurso is called the Alexander Bain Building, and there is an original Bain electric clock in the hall at Watten, between Wick and Thurso.

49. ALEXANDER GRAHAM BELL AND THE TELEPHONE

Alexander Graham Bell was born at 16 South Charlotte Street, on the corner of Charlotte Square, in Edinburgh, on 3 March 1847. His father and his grandfather were both authorities on elocution, and it wasn't long before the young Alexander was teaching people how to speak. He was enormously inventive, and not only made the first iron lung, but also bred special sheep with multiple nipples because he thought they would have more lambs. However, what makes him a legendary inventor is the telephone.

In 1863, at the age of sixteen, Alexander and his brother Melville began some serious research into how speech worked. They started with the anatomy of the mouth and throat and even examined the family cat (after it had died) so they could study the vocal cords in more detail. Studying the pitch of the vowel sounds, they imagined the throat and the mouth like two different-sized bottles. Each makes a different pitch, and they realised that the vowel sounds were a combination of two pitches. Their father, Melville senior, had spent years classifying vocal sounds and came up with a shorthand system called *Visible Speech*, where every sound was represented by a symbol. The idea was to teach the deaf to speak by putting all these sounds together.

They eventually made an elaborate speaking machine to test their theories. Later in 1863, Alexander went to Elgin near the Moray Firth in the north of Scotland to teach elocution at the Weston

Bell inaugurating the New York–Chicago telephone service on 18 October 1892.

House Academy, and there, in what is now a Comet store, he first conceived the idea of transmitting speech with electricity.

When Alexander's two brothers died in 1870, the family moved to North America. Alexander settled in Boston, the scientific and academic centre of America, and was soon using *Visible Speech* to teach the deaf. The idea of transmitting speech along a wire never left him, and though he knew little about electricity he knew a good deal about speech and sound. His years of research led him up a few blind alleys, but by 1875 he had come up with a simple receiver that could turn electricity into sound: in other words, a speaker. It was essentially a magnet glued to a diaphragm, and able to move within a coil of wire, so that a change of electric current in the coil would cause the magnet, and therefore also the diaphragm, to move in or out. Thus a varying electrical signal produced a varying sound wave from the speaker.

But he still needed a transmitter. He had no effective way of converting the sounds of the voice into an electric signal. What he needed, as his assistant Tom Watson put it, was to 'generate voice-shaped electric undulations'. He tried a few weird contraptions, including a diaphragm connected to a needle. As he spoke into it, the needle dipped in and out of a bowl of acid. The varying resistance produced a varying electric current from a battery. The great breakthrough came quite by accident on 2 June 1875. Bell and Watson were testing a circuit with one transmitter and two receivers in separate rooms, when Bell switched off the transmitter. Then he heard a note coming from the receiver in his room. Puzzled by this, he went through, and found Watson adjusting the other receiver. Bell realised that, with the transmitter turned off, the note must be coming from the other receiver acting as a transmitter – in other words, as a microphone. At that moment, the telephone was born.

By a fluke, Bell had discovered that the receiver could also work in reverse – instead of making sound when he sent electricity through it, it made electricity when he supplied sound, because the sound moved the diaphragm, the diaphragm moved the magnet in the coil and this generated electricity. Six months went by before he was able to send intelligible speech down the wire, and according to popular legend, and Bell's diary, the first words ever spoken on the telephone were, 'Mr Watson, come here;

I want to see you.' Rather peremptory, but no doubt the great man was excited, and no doubt Mr Watson jumped to it with alacrity.

Bell developed his system – he certainly needed a much better microphone – and submitted his patent on St Valentine's Day, 1876, just two hours before Elisha Gray, his main rival. The patent was granted on 7 March, and was one of the most valuable patents ever issued. Over 600 lawsuits followed before a Supreme Court decision ruled in Bell's favour in 1893. Meanwhile, Bell had made the telephone available to the public in 1877, when the Bell Telephone Company was created. Developments were swift; within a year the first telephone exchange was built in Connecticut and within ten years more than 150,000 people had telephones in the United States alone. Bell married Mabel, the deaf daughter of his financial partner, and signed nearly all of his stock over to her, keeping just ten shares for 'sentimental reasons'. Within three years the price of Bell Telephone Company shares soared from fifty dollars to over a thousand dollars. Alexander was finally a man of independent means.

Bell eventually built a large house in remote Nova Scotia, where the landscape and weather reminded him of Scotland. Here he continued his work with the deaf, including the young Helen Keller. He invented weird aircraft with wings based on triangles; he built a resuscitation device, the forerunner to the iron lung; and experimented with sheep. He had a peculiar notion that sheep with extra nipples would give birth to two or more lambs, and be more productive for farmers. He built Sheepville, a huge village of sheep pens, and spent years counting sheep nipples. The work continued for decades before the US state department announced that there was no link between extra nipples and extra lambs.

Alexander Graham Bell was kind and generous and gave much of his money and time to improving the lives of those around him. He died in 1922 and will be revered for his work with the deaf and celebrated for his invention of the telephone.

There's a plaque on the wall of the house where he was born, 16 South Charlotte Street, Edinburgh, and a little sign on a pillar in the Comet store in Elgin – and many telephone companies still carry the name of Bell.

50. HENRY HUNNINGS'S TELEPHONE MICROPHONE

York is an old Roman city, a centre of learning – and just the sort of place I expected to find heroic pioneers. Furthermore, in Victorian times clergymen often dabbled in science; they were well educated and reasonably well paid, and they often had time on their hands. However, I was surprised to discover that a major advance in telecommunications was made in the tiny village of Bolton Percy, a few miles west of York, by the curate there – a man called Henry Hunnings. Life in small villages often revolved around the church, and as curate Henry Hunnings was involved in weddings, funerals, and vital decisions such as whether to prevent the sexton from buying oil for the bells without the sanction of the churchwarden.

Meanwhile in Boston, Massachusetts, an expatriate Scot called Alexander Graham Bell was working with deaf people, and trying to develop hearing aids, such as the system of *Visible Speech* invented by his father. As an extension of this work, he looked for ways to transmit speech along wires, and in 1875 invented the telephone.

Unfortunately it didn't work very well to begin with, because at both ends he had what we would call a speaker, and speakers aren't really sensitive enough for the voice; so he had to shout as loud as he could to be heard in the next room and, although exciting, it wasn't very practical. Then along came Thomas Alva Edison, possibly the greatest inventor of all time, who produced a mouthpiece made out of compressed soot (known as lampblack). Unfortunately that didn't work terribly well either.

At this point Henry Hunnings had a brilliant idea. We don't know how he knew about the telephone and the problems of getting speech into it, but he thought that maybe Edison should have used not soot, but bigger chunks of carbon. So Hunnings got hold of some charcoal and crushed it to make big granules. He put the granules between two thin metal plates or diaphragms to make a sandwich, and connected a battery across the two diaphragms. The idea was that the pressure of sound waves from the voice would push the diaphragms together and lower the electrical resistance, so more current would flow in the circuit.

That's the principle of the Hunnings microphone. The compressing of the chunks of carbon lowers the resistance, so that each bit of voice causes a pulse of current to flow in the circuit, and this can be sent as a signal along a wire. The weird thing is that anyone who knew anything about electricity couldn't possibly have invented this, because it seems to be obvious that no voice pressure could be high enough – you'd never shout loudly enough to be able to move those great chunks of carbon about. However, he was confident enough to patent his device in September 1878.

Hunnings tested his microphone on the telegraph wires between York and Darlington, and held a public demonstration of the 'micro-telephone' (price 15 guineas) at Cleveland Institute of Engineers, and it turned out to work extremely well. So well, in fact, that Alexander Graham Bell sued Hunnings – and lost. Eventually Bell bought the rights from Henry Hunnings for a thousand pounds. Not bad for a humble curate living in Bolton Percy.

And what an invention! The carbon-granule microphone remained in use until it was replaced by electronic systems in the 1980s; thus, in every telephone handset, the improbable genius of Henry Hunnings lived on for more than a hundred years.

If you have a little electrical meter you can easily make a model to see how the carbon-granule microphone works. First make a teaspoonful of carbon granules from a barbecue briquette (or artist's charcoal) by bashing it with a hammer. Lay a thin layer of granules on a 2p or 50p coin. Lay another coin on top. Make a circuit with a battery, the two coin-diaphragms, and the meter, set to measure current at its most sensitive setting. Then, while watching the meter, press on the top coin with your thumb, and see how the current increases with the pressure.

Bolton Percy is a pretty village with a lovely church, and a phone box within sight, but there is no plaque to commemorate the forgotten curate.

51. JOHN LOGIE BAIRD, INVENTOR OF UNDERSOCKS AND THE TELEVISION

Quite a lot of these heroes have been loners, working away on their own with inadequate resources and no recognition from the authorities until it was too late. But in the twentieth century, most science is done by professionals, often in universities or proper laboratories. So it is rather surprising to find that one of the greatest inventions of this century was made by a man literally starving in a garret. Using his own pathetic finances he beat huge organisations in many countries to one of the holy grails of engineering – the ability to send moving pictures from one place to another.

The inventor of television was the son of a Scottish minister in Helensburgh, north-west of Glasgow, and his name was John Logie Baird. Baird was a sickly boy, and was dogged by ill-health all his life. He was declared unfit for army service, and recurring bronchitis cut short many of his business ventures. Unable to pursue more conventional careers, he devoted his energies to the passion he developed at the age of thirteen – for television. As a boy he was already inventive. He rigged up a telephone exchange between his parents' house and those of his friends Whimster, Bruce, Norwell, and Wadsworth. It all came to a disastrous end one stormy night when one of the wires dangled too low and lifted a passing cab-man clean out of his seat.

The idea of television was not new. Even the word television had been coined in 1900 when JLB was only twelve years old, and he must have dreamed about the possibilities. The key discovery had been that the element Selenium is photoelectric – its electrical resistance changes as the light falling on it goes from bright to dim, an effect which is used in the light meter. Around the world people wondered whether this phenomenon could somehow do for vision what the telephone had done for speech. So the race to develop television was on.

Not surprisingly, although John's dad was a minister in the church and wanted his son to follow in his footsteps, John had other ideas and enrolled instead in the Royal Glasgow College of Technology to study electrical engineering. By an amazing coincidence, a fellow student was John Reith who was to become the first director-general of the BBC. The two did not get on. Unfit for service when the war broke out in 1914, Baird spent his time instead maintaining the Glasgow electricity supply, plunging large parts of the city into darkness on one occasion when he connected an experiment in artificial diamond production across the terminals of a power station.

After the war, Baird began to show an entrepreneurial streak. With no career, he turned to commerce and invented the 'Baird Patent Undersock'. These wonderful things were supposed to be worn under your socks, to keep the feet warm and dry, and so prevent rising damp! They were treated with borax, although Baird apparently once revealed that the secret lining was old newspapers. Baird made the socks himself, writing testimonials from fictitious satisfied customers, and then sold them round the stores of Glasgow. His marketing stunts included 'the first sandwich women in Glasgow'. It sounds like a bit of a joke –

but at one time he was making £200 a week. He also sold soap and boot-polish, until his bronchitis forced him to give up. Hoping for a healthier climate, he headed for Trinidad where his first commercial ventures failed, so instead he set up a jam factory. He carried on in the same vein on his return to Britain until his health was so bad that he virtually retired to Hastings, aged thirty-four.

This was 1922, and Baird may have been experimenting with television all along. He now decided to devote himself to it. Television was much more difficult than radio. A single microphone can pick up all the sound in a room and convert it into an electrical signal, which can be fed down a wire. A single photocell can do the same thing for light – but all you would get is a reading of the average brightness of the scene – not very interesting. You could have thousands of these cells, one in each part of the picture, connected by wires to thousands of light-bulbs or whatever in your receiver, but that is completely impractical and could never work over radio. In all his experiments Baird was constantly thinking about how his pictures might be delivered, and was careful not to generate

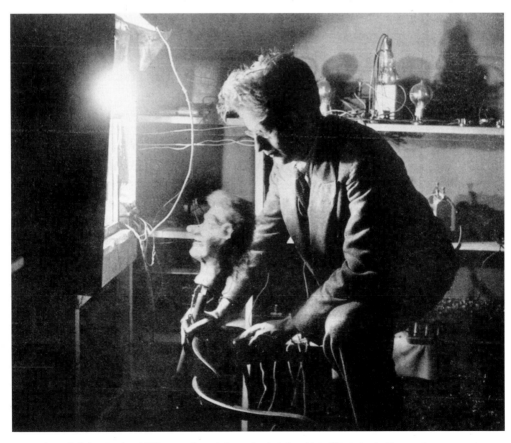

Because he worked alone Baird used 'Bill', a ventriloquist's dummy head, as the subject of his early television experiments.

more information than the medium (literally the medium wave in his day) could handle.

Baird was by no means the only television experimenter, and he made use of whatever existing technology seemed to work. A German engineer called Paul Nipkow worked out in 1884 how to transmit pictures using a single photocell. He realised that you could scan points in the picture one after the other and then somehow reassemble them at the other end. If you could do this quickly enough you might fool the eye into seeing moving pictures. The 'Nipkow Disc' remained a central part of all Baird's mechanical television experiments and consisted simply of a spinning disc with a spiral of holes punched in it. Placed in front of a picture, the effect was of a hole scanning gradually over the picture, first down one line, then the next and so on. Baird realised that this scanning system was key – at any time there is only one hole scanning the picture, so you only need one photocell behind the disc to measure the light coming through.

This is the sort of system he used in Hastings, in his room over an artificial flower shop, from 1922. At the other end, the receiver, you had an almost identical machine – called by Baird the 'Televisor'. But instead of a photocell, there was a lamp whose brightness varied in proportion to the signal from the transmitter. Crucially he worked out how to get the transmitter and the Televisor synchronised. He first televised a Maltese cross, and although the picture quality was poor – just a black and white silhouette – what impressed people was the fact that these were moving pictures.

He had found a system that could scan a picture and transmit enough information to fool the eye.

In 1924 Baird moved to London, and in March 1925 Mr Gordon Selfridge jnr, of the Selfridges department store, heard about the experiments and suggested a public demonstration in the shop; he would pay Baird £25 a week for three weeks. It was the world's first public demonstration of television. People flocked to see his crude pictures, made up of just 30 lines – today we use 625. Nevertheless, it was hailed as a great success, and some visitors worried that since this thing could send pictures through walls, this could mark the end of privacy. Despite his amazing achievement, Baird soon ran out of money. People who visited him were shocked to see him working in carpet slippers and no socks. He persuaded some Scottish relations to invest, which let him continue work on the photocell.

He couldn't improve on the black and white image – he wanted shades of grey. At one point he had been so desperate for a new device that he persuaded an eye surgeon to give him a fresh human eye so that he could try an extract from the retina, but it didn't help. Finally, on 2 October 1925, Baird sat 'Bill', a ventriloquist's dummy, in front of the transmitter so that he could watch the Televisor. What he saw was amazing – a face, in reasonable detail. Baird rushed downstairs and grabbed William Taynton, an office boy working on the floor below, and sat him in front of the transmitter. But Baird saw nothing from the next room. Puzzled, he returned to the transmitter to find that William had

An original Baird 'Televisor'. The label carried Baird's signature and the slogan 'The Eyes of the World'.

moved his chair back from the transmitter as he couldn't stand the ultra-bright light Baird had to use. Half a crown solved the problem. Baird told him to open his mouth and move his head – so William was the first person to be televised – though several other people claim the honour.

Baird went public the following summer, inviting fifty scientists and others to his Soho attic; they queued in the street and on the stairs as only five at a time could fit in. In the USA Radio News confirmed that 'Mr Baird has definitely and indisputably given a demonstration of real television. It is the first time in history that this has been done in any part of the world.' He soon managed to send pictures via the telephone, and in 1928 across the Atlantic by radio. It is claimed that

although he already had the ability to produce far superior pictures, he revealed only the 30-line transmissions because nothing with more information could have been squeezed through a telephone line.

Baird had done it. Although most of the technology – like the Nipkow Disc – had been invented by other people, only Baird had made television work, despite the attempts of huge corporations in America and elsewhere. He became a bit of a celebrity, especially when he finally got the BBC to agree to a broadcast trial. Amazingly, they didn't seem to be interested at first: they had a system of sending still pictures by wireless – rather like having a fax attached to your radio. Eventually the postmaster-general, who supported Baird, insisted that the BBC test Baird's system. Regular transmissions started less than thrillingly on Monday 30 September 1929 with a message from the President of the Board of Trade, who said that 'This new industry will provide employment for large numbers of our people and will prove the prestige of British creative energy.'

For the first six months, sound and vision were sent alternately, as only one transmitter was available. From 31 March 1930 sound and vision broadcasts were possible, and a Televisor was installed in 10 Downing Street for Prime Minister Ramsay MacDonald and his family. MacDonald immediately realised what television was all about. On 5 April 1930 he wrote a wonderful letter:

> Dear Mr Baird,
>
> I must thank you very warmly for the television instrument you have put into Downing Street. What a marvellous discovery you have made! When I look at the transmissions I feel that the most wonderful miracle is being done under my eye . . . You have put something in my room which will never let me forget how strange is the world – and how unknown. Again and again I thank you.
>
> With kindest regards,
>
> J. Ramsay MacDonald

On 3 June 1931 Baird triumphantly televised the Derby from Epsom. It seemed that television had arrived, and Baird was the man who had done it. But of course that isn't the end of the story. We don't watch television through spinning discs, even though Baird quickly produced much better pictures including colour and 3D television.

At the same time Baird was making mechanical television, another system was being developed. The cathode ray tube had been invented in 1897. We now call cathode rays electrons, and they are fired from the back of the tube. You can make them light up the front of the tube and you can steer them electrically to scan in lines – like the holes in the disc, but with far more lines than Baird's mechanical television could achieve. The cathode ray tube was adapted for the television camera as well. The BBC ran twin trials of a Baird mechanical 240-line system, and the Marconi-EMI electronic system at 405 lines. In 1937 the Baird system was switched off: electronics had won.

All television shut down during the war, and although Baird kept working at new ideas, he died in 1946 – the year television really took off in Britain.

There are conflicting views of Baird. Some regard him as a brilliant but misguided pioneer, who backed the wrong system and rightly lost out to electronic television. Others point out many experiments that Baird himself made which could have led to – some say did result in – a Baird electronic system far better than the one we ended up with. That he lost out is thanks to the terms of the 1937 trial and the government backing a system under American pressure. This is still controversial, and new information is still being uncovered. Whatever the final conclusion, no one can take away the fact that John Logie Baird was the first person in the world to demonstrate the transmission of moving images from one place to another – television.

There is a bust of John Logie Baird at his birthplace, Helensburgh. It looks wistfully out to sea. There is also a plaque on the house in which he was born in West Argyle Street in Glasgow. There is a memorial at Central Hotel, Glasgow, the site of an early transmission, and a blue plaque at 22 Frith Street, where his first demonstration took place.

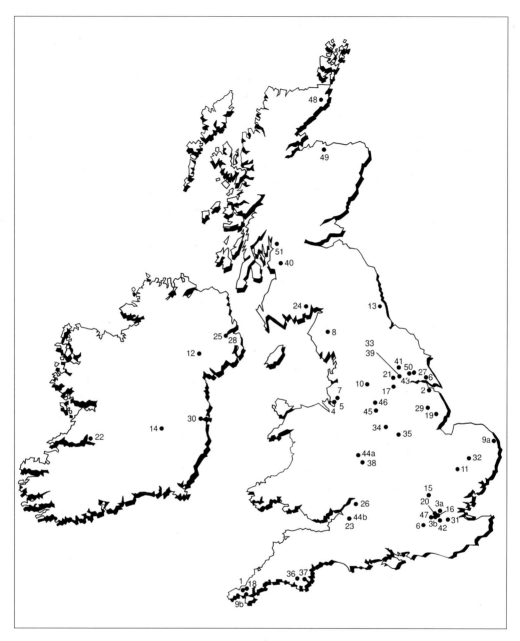

Map of Local Heroes.

Key

1. William Bickford (Tuckingmill)
2. John Harrison (Barrow-on-Humber)
3a. Charles Babbage (Bloomsbury)
3b. Ada Lovelace (St James's Square)
4. Frank Hornby (Liverpool)
5. Arthur Doodson (Liverpool)
6. Barnes Wallis (Weybridge)
7. Alastair Pilkington (St Helens)
8. William Brownrigg (Derwentwater)
9a. George Manby (Yarmouth)
9b. Henry Trengrouse (Helston)
10. Richard Towneley (Burnley)
11. Robert Fitzroy (Bury St Edmunds)
12. Thomas Romney Robinson (Armagh)
13. Lewis Fry Richardson (Newcastle)
14. John Tyndall (Leighlinbridge)
15. Francis Bacon (St Albans)
16. Nicholas de Chemant (Soho)
17. Joseph Bramah (Barnsley)
18. William Murdock (Redruth)
19. Joseph Banks (Revesby)
20. William Banting (London)
21. Margaret McMillan (Bradford)
22. Joe Sheridan (Shannon Airport)
23. George Pocock (Bristol)
24. Kirkpatrick MacMillan (Thornhill)
25. John Boyd Dunlop (Belfast)
26. Mikael Pedersen (Dursley)
27. Joseph Aloysius Hansom (York)
28. Harry Ferguson (Belfast)
29. William Ashbee Tritton (Lincoln)
30. William Petty (Dublin)
31. Cornelis Drebbel (Eltham)
32. Benjamin Wiseman (Diss)
33. John Smeaton (Leeds)
34. Richard Arkwright (Cromford)
35. Edmund Cartwright (Goadby Marwood)
36. Thomas Savery (Modbury)
37. Thomas Newcomen (Dartmouth)
38. James Watt (Birmingham)
39. Matthew Murray (Leeds)
40. Robert Stirling (Galston)
41. John Metcalfe (Knaresborough)
42. Eleanor Coade (Lambeth)
43. Joseph Aspdin (Leeds)
44a. Thomas Telford (Telford)
44b. John Loudon McAdam (Bristol)
45. Joseph Paxton (Chatsworth)
46. Donald Bailey (Rotherham)
47. Samuel Morland (Vauxhall)
48. Alexander Bain (Wick)
49. Alexander Graham Bell (Elgin)
50. Henry Hunnings (Bolton Percy)
51. John Logie Baird (Helensburgh)

CHRONOLOGY

LOCAL HEROES		HISTORIC EVENTS	
c. 800	Alcuin's *Proposites ad Acuendes Juvenes*	Charlemagne crowned Holy Roman Emperor on Christmas Day	800
		Mary Tudor	**1553**
1557	Robert Recorde invents equals sign		
		Elizabeth I	**1558**
		William Shakespeare born	1564
		James I	**1603**
		Gunpowder Plot	1605
1610	Galileo observes moons of Jupiter		
		Authorised Version of the Bible	1611
		Witches of Pendle tried	1612
1614	John Napier's book of logarithms		
1620	Cornelis Drebbel's submarine	Pilgrim Fathers sail to New England	1620
		Charles I	**1625**
1628	Wm Harvey's book on circulation		
1642	Galileo dies		
1642	Isaac Newton born	English Civil War	1642
		Taj Mahal completed	1652
		Charles II	**1660**
		Royal Society founded	1660
1662	William Petty invents catamaran		
		Great Plague	1665
1666	Isaac Newton's *annus mirabilis*	Great Fire of London	1666
1670	S. Morland's *tuba stentoro-phonica*		
1672	Isaac Newton's letter on the spectrum		
		Wren's Greenwich Observatory	1675
1677	Richard Towneley records rainfall		
1681	S. Morland *magister mechanicorum*		
		James II	**1685**
1687	John Clayton rector at Crofton		
1687	Isaac Newton's *Principia*		
		William III and Mary II	**1688**
		Bank of England founded	1691
1698	T. Savery's patent for 'raiseing water'		
1698	Winstanley's Eddystone lighthouse		
		Anne	**1702**
1703	Eddystone lighthouse destroyed		
		Sir Clowdisley Shovell hits Scillies	1707
1709	Abraham Darby makes iron with coke		
1711	N. Saunderson Lucasian Professor		
1712	First Newcomen engine, Dudley	Last witchcraft execution, England	1712

		George I	1714
		Fahrenheit's temperature scale	1714
		Walpole first Prime Minister	1721
		George II	1727
1733	John Kay invents flying shuttle		
		Britain adopts Gregorian calendar	1752
1754	Joseph Black's thesis published		
1757	John Gough, blind philosopher, born		
1759	John Smeaton's Eddystone lighthouse		
1759	John Harrison's marine chronometer		
		George III	1760
1762	Matthew Boulton's Soho Manufactory		
1765	Blind Jack starts making roads		
		Lunar Society of Birmingham	1766
1768	Pinchbeck's nocturnal remembrancer		
1768	Wm Cookworthy's porcelain patent		
1769	R. Arkwright patents water frame		
1769	Eleanor Coade sets up stone business		
1769	J. Cook and J. Banks sail to Tahiti	Transit of Venus observed	1769
1769	James Watt's first steam engine patent		
1771	Joseph Priestley makes oxygen	Richard Arkwright's cotton mill	1771
1772	Brownrigg & Franklin, oil on water		
1773	John Harrison gets reward		
1774	Maskelyne measures mass of Earth	Boulton and Watt partnership	1774
1775	William Withering discovers digitalis		
1775	Charles Hutton invents contour lines	American War of Independence	1775
1775	First WC patent: Alexander Cumming		
1775	Watt's steam engine works!		
1775	John Wilkinson's boring machine		
1778	Joseph Bramah's water-closet patent	James Cook discovers Hawaii	1778
1779	James Watt's copying machine		
1782	William Watts makes lead shot	Montgolfiers build air balloon	1782
1783	John Michell describes a black hole		
1783	Benjamin Wiseman's windmill		
1784	Wm Murdock's model steam loco		
1785	Edmund Cartwright's power loom		
1787	John Dalton sees aurora		
1788	Edward Jenner writes about cuckoos		
1788	G. White's *Natural History of Selborne*		
		French Revolution	1789
1790	Joseph Bramah's unpickable lock		
1791	John Barber patents gas turbine		
		Metric system introduced in France	1795
1796	Edward Jenner vaccinates J. Phipps		
1796	Geo. Cayley's whirling-arm machine		
1797	Joseph Bramah's beer engine		
1797	de Chemant's stove-cum-dining-table		
1798	H. Cavendish measures mass of Earth	Malthus's essay on population	1798
1798	Humphry Davy tries laughing gas		
1799	J. Black dies without spilling milk	Rosetta Stone found in Egypt	1799
1799	The flower of physic is Withering		
1800	Beaufort seriously wounded in battle		

1800	W.H. Wollaston's camera lucida		
1801	Richard Trevithick's steam carriage		
1802	William Murdock lights Soho with gas		
1803	J. Dalton introduces atomic weights		
1804	R. Trevithick's Penydaren locomotive		
1805	Telford builds Pont Cysyllte aquaduct		
1806	George Parker Bidder born Dartmoor		
1808	First use of Manby's mortar		
1811	Mary Anning finds ichthyosaurus		
1812	Sarah Guppy's improved tea urn		
1814	T. Young deciphers Rosetta Stone		
1815	J.L. McAdam starts building roads		
1815	W. Smith's geological map of Britain	Battle of Waterloo	1815
1816	David Brewster's kaleidoscope		
1816	Robert Stirling's heat engine		
1820	First sewage pollution of Windermere	George IV	1820
1821	William Buckland finds hyena bones		
1822	Babbage's model difference engine		
1823	Mary Anning finds first plesiosaur		
1824	Joe Aspdin patents Portland Cement		
1825	Goldsworthy Gurney's steam carriage		
1826	David Douglas sends Douglas Fir		
1826	Telford's Menai Bridge opened		
1828	Mary Anning finds first pterodactyl		
1828	George Green's mathematical essay		
1828	George Pocock's charvolant		
1830	Edwin Budding's lawnmower	William IV	1830
1831	Fitzroy and Darwin sail in *Beagle*	British Association for the Advancement	
1831	William Bickford invents safety fuse	of Science founded	1831
1831	Sarah Guppy's ingenious bedstead		
1832	Joseph Aloysius Hansom patents a cab		
1833	G. Boole's vision in a field in Doncaster		
1833	T.R. Robinson's cup anemometer		
1834	E.L. Berthon's screw propeller		
1837	Thomas Edmondson's railway ticket	Victoria	1837
1839	Armagh found 2 feet further west		
1839	Goldsworthy Gurney's Bude light	Penny post in England	1839
1839	Kirkpatrick MacMillan's bicycle		
1840	W. Whewell invents the word scientist	Indian Mutiny	1840
1841	J. Whitworth's universal screw threads	Brunel's GWR reaches Bristol	1841
1842	Wm Coppin launches Great Northern		
1842	A. Lovelace's computer programmes		
1843	Alexander Bain's fax machine		
1845	G.P. Bidder's railway swing bridge		
1845	R. Thompson patents pneumatic tyre		
1846	C.P. Smyth Astron. Royal for Scotland		
1847	Brunel's atmospheric railway opens		
1847	J. Joule's mechanical equivalent of heat		
1848	J. Stringfellow achieves powered flight		
		Cholera kills 55,000 in Britain	1849
1851	Joseph Paxton builds Crystal Palace	Great Exhibition, London	1851

1853	Geo. Cayley's *New Flyer* carries man		
1854	Florence Nightingale sails for Crimea		
		'Great stink' debated in Parliament	1858
1859	Charles Darwin's *Origin of Species*		
1860	Henry Moule patents earth-closet		
1860	C. Pullinger's perpetual mouse-trap		
1861	Thomas Crapper sets up as plumber		
1861	Fitzroy invents weather forecast		
1862	Alexander Parkes produces parkesine		
1863	Wm Banting's *Letter on Corpulence*		
1863	James Clerk Maxwell's colour photo	London Underground	1863
		Pasteurisation	1864
		Mendel's law of heredity	1865
1866	John Getty McGee's Ulster overcoat	*Great Eastern* lays Atlantic cable	1866
1867	John Tyndall superintendent of RI		
1872	Kelvin & Tower invent tide machine		
1875	Alexander Graham Bell's telephone		
	SS *Bessemer's* maiden and last voyage		
	William Marwood hangs first victim		
1877	John Jeyes patents Jeyes Fluid		
1878	Hunnings's telephone microphone		
1879	G.W. Garrett launches *Resurgam*		
1889	John Boyd Dunlop's pneumatic tyre		
		Diesel internal combustion engine	1892
1893	Mikael Pedersen's tension bikes	Henry Ford makes first car	1893
		X-rays discovered by W. Röntgen	1895
1896	Fred Lanchester's petrol-driven car	Nobel Prizes founded	1896
1896	L. Pedrazzolli's swimming umbrellas	1st modern Olympic Games Athens	1896
1897	Dr Gaddes's automatic egg-boiler		
1900	John Milne's seismology laboratory	Quantum theory, Max Planck	1900
1901	Frank Hornby's Meccano	**Edward VII**	1901
1902	T. Anderson snaps Mt Pelée eruption		
1904	H. Ayrton's paper to Royal Society		
		Albert Einstein's special relativity	1905
1907	Margaret McMillan's school dinners		
		George V	1910
1916	First Tritton tanks see action		
1919	L.F. Richardson's psychology of war		
1932	G. Malloch's salmon gaff, etc.		
		Edward VIII, George VI	1936
1937	Ted Wright finds first Ferriby boat		
1941	Sir Donald Bailey's bridge		
1942	Joe Sheridan invents Irish coffee		
1943	Barnes Wallis's bouncing bombs		
1944	Arthur Doodson predicts D-Day tides		
1946	Ferguson's TE20 – the 'Wee Fergie'		
1947	Dennis Gabor's imaginary hologram		
1948	Nicholas Kove's first Airfix kit		
1948	Richardson's parsnip experiment		
1952	Pilkington's float glass process	**Elizabeth II**	1952
1958	Mackereth's pneumatic bottom corer		

FURTHER READING

The best single source of information about our heroes is *The Dictionary of National Biography* published by Oxford University Press. We always look in *DNB*, and find many of our heroes there. What is more, most of the entries are reasonably short and accurate.

The series of books by Samuel Smiles and L.T.C. Rolt are also excellent sources, and easy to read: Smiles, *Lives of the Engineers* (including Smeaton, Metcalfe, Telford, Boulton and Watt); *Self Help*; Rolt, *Thomas Telford*; *James Watt*; *Great Engineers*, Bell, 1962; Allen & Rolt, *The Steam Engine of Thomas Newcomen*.

For a gazetteer of scientific hero sites, try Trevor I. Williams, *Our Scientific Heritage*, Sutton, 1996, or Charles Tanford & Jacqueline Reynolds, *A Travel Guide to Scientific Sites of the British Isles*, Wiley, 1995.

For an analysis of innovations, G.I. Brown, *The Guinness History of Inventions*, Guinness, 1996, Donald Clarke, *The Encyclopedia of Inventions*, Marshall Cavendish, 1977, or Patrick Robertson, *The Shell Book of Firsts*, Ebury Press, 1974.

For an overview, see T.K. Derry & Trevor I. Williams, *A Short History of Technology*, Dover, 1960, George Basalla, *The Evolution of Technology*, Cambridge University Press, 1988, or Donald Cardwell, *The Fontana History of Technology*, Fontana, 1994.

INDIVIDUAL HEROES

Alison Kelly, *Mrs Coade's Stone*, Self Publishing Association (Lloyds Bank Chambers, Upton-on-Severn, Worcs), 1990.

Dava Sobel, *Longitude* (John Harrison), Fourth Estate, 1996.

Ronald Frank Tiltman, *Baird of Television. The Life Story of John Logie Baird*, Seeley, Service & Co., 1933.

Tom McArthur & Peter Waddell, *Vision Warrior, The Hidden Achievement of John Logie Baird*, Scottish Falcon, 1990.

Sermons, Soap and Television, Royal Television Society.

G. Irving, *The Devil on Wheels* (Kirkpatrick Macmillan), 1986.

Markku Peltonen (ed.), *The Cambridge Companion to Bacon*, Cambridge, 1996.

Robert Sier, *Rev. Robert Stirling DD, Inventor of the Heat Economiser and Stirling Cycle Engine*, L.A. Mair, 1995.

Doris Langley Moore, *Ada, Countess of Lovelace*, 1977.

Anthony Hyman, *Charles Babbage, Pioneer of the Computer*, 1982.

M.P. Gould, *Frank Hornby*, 1915.

Sir Frank Whittle, *Jet*, Pan, 1957.

James Mackay, *Sounds out of Silence, a Life of Alexander Graham Bell*, Edinburgh Mainstream, 1997.

Dixon's *Literary Life of W. Brownrigg*, 1801.

A. Mansbridge, *Margaret McMillan*, Prophet and Pioneer, 1932.

Jean McClintock, *History of the Pneumatic Tyre*, 1923.

INDEX